From The Nail To The Key

The *Fundamental Theology of Pope Francis*

Edited by

MICHELINA TENACE

Together with lecturers
from the Department of Fundamental
Theology,
Pontifical Gregorian University

COVENTRY
PRESS

Nowadays, fundamental theology as a place of encounter and dialogue between believer and non-believers has a fascinating teacher and witness: Francis, who is the pope of a Church *going forth* to the existential peripheries of the women and men of today.

Faced with a theology that too often is dry and *does not speak* to the concrete life of the people, a kind of *nail to suck on*, he proposes and dreams of theology as a *key that opens* the door to the Church's treasure to then offer it as a gift to humanity: theology as a place of encounter and fellowship.

Lecturers from the Department of Fundamental Theology at the Pontifical Gregorian University have welcomed the challenge to *do* theology together, in the Church and for the world, starting out from the Magisterium of Pope Francis.

Published in Australia by
Copyright © Coventry Press 2019
Coventry Press
33 Scoresby Road
Bayswater Vic. 3153
Australia

Translated into English by Salesians of Don Bosco of the Province of Mary Help of Christians of Australia and The Pacific

ISBN 9780648230366

First edition November 2017 by LEV
First reprint January 2018 by LEV

© Copyright 2017 -- Libreria Editrice Vaticana
  00120 Città del Vaticano
  Tel. 06 698.81032 - Fax 06 698.84716
  E-mail: commerciale.lev@spc.va

All rights reserved. Other than for the purposes and subject to the conditions prescribed under the Copyright Act, no part of this publication may be reproduced, stored in a retrieval system, or transmitted in any form or by any means, electronic, mechanical, photocopying, recording or otherwise, without the prior permission of the publisher.

Scripture quotations are from the New Revised Standard Version Bible, copyright 1989, Division of Christian Education of the National Council of the Churches of Christ in the United States of America. Used by permission. All rights reserved.

Cataloguing-in-Publication entry is available from the National Library of Australia http:/catalogue.nla.gov.au/.

Printed in Australia
www.coventrypress.com.au

Cover:
A glimpse of St Peter's Square from inside the Basilica at the Vatican
© 'L'osservatore Romano' photographic service

Contents

Michelina Tenace
Introduction. From the 'nail that fastens' to the 'key that opens': the fundamental theology of Pope Francis 7

Joseph Xavier
The dynamics of faith in Pope Francis' thinking .. 21

Maria Carmen Aparicio Valls
The significant word. 39

Ferenc Patsch
Revelation, context, truth.
    The magisterium of Pope Francis at a time of transition 51

Stella Morra
A faithful people among peoples: elements of fundamental ecclesiology 79

Andrew Downing
History and the open horizon of the future 93

Nicolas Steeves
'An imaginative Pope's imaginative theology!' ... 105

Gerard Whelan
Pope Francis' theological method 117

James Corkery
Francis, heir and innovator: an Argentinian Pope and Jesuit in the post-conciliar tradition... 137

Michelina Tenace

INTRODUCTION

From the 'nail that fastens' to the 'key that opens': the fundamental theology of Pope Francis

On 10 April 2014, the Pontifical Gregorian University was received by the Holy Father, Pope Francis, in the Paul VI auditorium. On that occasion, the Pope summed up the task of theology and the characteristics of the true theologian in just a few words. Theology is about creating a true 'evangelical' movement that goes from the centre to the periphery and from the periphery to the centre, 'according to the logic of God who reaches the centre from the peripheries in order to return to the peripheries.'[1]

From this image of theology forever shifting between centre and periphery, there also emerges an image of the theologian whose theology will be 'all the more fruitful and effective the more fully it is animated by love for Christ and for the Church.'[2] Centre and periphery. Study and prayer.

---

1 FRANCIS, *Address to the Community of the Pontifical Gregorian University and associates from the Pontifical Biblical Institute* (10-04-2014).
2 *IBID.*

The theologian must be involved in 'transmitting knowledge and offering a key for vital comprehension, not a heap of notions unconnected to one another.' The Pontiff added that the Church today has no need of 'a synthesis but of a spiritual atmosphere of research and certainty based on the truths of reason and of faith.'[3]

Implicit here is an accusation levelled at a certain kind of theology and a certain way of being a theologian: there is a kind of theology which congratulates itself on being complete and conclusive thinking. It points to a 'mediocre' theologian suffering from an 'ecclesiastical illness' which does the Church so much ill. It is like a thinker who is affected by a 'disgusting narcissism.'[4]

The message was addressed to a Pontifical University with a Faculty of Theology which has more students than any other and which, over the centuries, has formed theologians for the entire Church. The Pope's words describing the type of theology and theologians the Church does not need today resonated, then, with particular force that day.

At the end of the audience, the Holy Father greeted the academic and administrative authorities, the deans and heads of departments.

---
3   Ibid.
4   Ibid.

Fr François-Xavier Dumortier SJ, the then Rector of the University, paused to present the Head of the Department of Fundamental Theology. It was here that Pope Francis, almost with compassion, used an expression which sounded full of meaning in the context of the address he had just given: 'Fundamental Theology! It's like sucking on a nail!' He had only just uttered his words on the type of theology that is an 'ecclesiastical illness' that is so 'disgusting' and the type of theologians affected by this 'disgusting narcissism' because they have become mediocre thinkers 'who [are] satisfied with [their] complete and conclusive thought .'[5]

There has been, and perhaps still is the kind of fundamental theology that really has been presented as a 'nail to suck on': a disgusting, worthless and boring thing. A theology which, due to the arrogance of knowledge closed in on itself, has encountered aridity and pride in the theologian 'who thinks [he] can reflect on God' with a hard heart: 'aridity of heart — how unpleasant it is when the heart becomes arid and believes itself capable of reflecting on God in that aridity, how many mistakes! — pride, even ambition.'[6]

---

5 IBID.
6 FRANCIS, *Address to members of the International Theological Commission* (6-12-2013)

As is his wont, Pope Francis was speaking from experience on that day too, and would explain it on another occasion.[7] 'Those of my generation ... were educated in a decadent scholasticism,' that is, they studied theology only from manuals. This way of doing theology 'provoked a casuistic attitude' to resolving problems. What was in the books was more real than what was happening in life. The 'great scholastic,' the 'great Thomas,' was a man who 'takes life into account.' 'In thinking of the human being, the Church should strive for genius, not decadence.' And again: 'When does a formulation of thought cease to be valid? When it loses sight of the human.'[8]

The word 'nail' appears in the title of this book on Pope Francis' Fundamental Theology to recall the context in which he uttered it.

So, what fundamental theology does the Church have need of?

Not of a nail that fastens, but of a key that opens!

---

[7] As reported in the paragraph, words and sentences from: FRANCIS' 'Have Courage and Prophetic Audacity. Dialogue of Pope Francis with the Jesuits gathered in the 36th General Congregation,' available at https://jesuits.org/assets/publications/file/gc36-dialogue_of_pope_francis_english.pdf. (originally in *La Civiltà Cattolica* 3995/IV, (10-12-2106) 421-422).

[8] End of the quotation from *Civiltà Cattolica* 2016.

Introduction

The above-quoted addresses and discourses help us understand that when he is speaking about theology, in reality Pope Francis is often referring to fundamental theology. And when the Pontiff is describing the theologian, he is really revealing himself without deliberately intending to do so. Therefore, we make bold as to say that today, fundamental theology has a fascinating teacher and witness: Pope Francis, the Pope of fundamental theology for the third millennium. His is a theology that opens, like a key – opens from Rome toward the Churches, and from the Churches toward Rome. It is 'threshold theology', an outlet that allows us to go from the centre to the periphery and from the periphery to the centre. An open theology. 'The good theologian and philosopher has an open, that is, an incomplete thought, always open to the *maius* of God and of the truth, always in development.' The true theologian is one who has a theology which integrates with 'missionary commitment, with fraternal charity and sharing with the poor, with care of the interior life in relationship with the Lord.'[9]

This is how Pope Francis expresses his fundamental theology!

---

9 FRANCIS, *Address to the Community of the Pontifical Gregorian University*.

From the nail that fastens to the key that opens. This, then, is how the title we have chosen for this book is to be understood. Fundamental theology should open up to the world, to the other, to dialogue. Open! We are struck by the frequency of the word 'open' in Pope Francis' addresses. The invitation to be open is a question of vocation, otherwise, among believers 'we risk getting used to closing doors.'[10]

Being open means running a new risk: that of encountering the other, which makes us afraid. The Pope told students and lecturers at the Faculty of Theology in Sardinia: 'Never be afraid of encounter, of dialogue, of comparisons … the very moment in history which we are living urges us *to seek and find paths of hope* that open our society to new horizons.'[11]

But in openness, the theologian will also find him or herself faced sooner or later with two temptations: given all the negativity one finds, there is the temptation to condemn the lot and revert to the past as if it were better; the temptation, that is, to seek refuge in sterile 'conservatism or fundamentalism.' But there is another temptation just as dangerous: to plunge into everything without

---

10 Francis, 'Have Courage and Prophetic Audacity'
11 Francis, *Address to students and professors of the Faculty of Theology in Sardinia* (22-09-2013)

discernment, accepting everything as if novelty were already something good of itself.

The true theologian is not a backward-looking conservative who justifies a closed approach by the need to be faithful to the Tradition; nor is this theologian someone who adapts to the world, justifying this adaption with pastoral necessity.

'To overcome these temptations, the path to take is reflection, taking the ecclesial Tradition and reality very seriously, getting them to dialogue.'[12]

In the past, theologians engaged in doctrine and theologians engaged in pastoral ministry faced off against one another. This opposition needs to be overcome because it is harmful: 'false opposition between theology and pastoral ministry; between the believer's reflection and the believer's life; life, then, which makes no room for reflection and reflection which makes no room for life. The great Fathers of the Church, Irenaeus, Augustine, Basil, Ambrose just to mention a few, were great theologians because they were great pastors.'[13]

If 'the encounter between doctrine and pastoral ministry is not optional [but] constitutive

---

12 FRANCIS, *Video message of the Holy Father to the International Congress of Theology at the Pontifical Catholic University Argentina*. (13-09-2015).
13 FRANCIS, *Video message of the Holy Father to the International Congress of Theology*

of a theology that intends being ecclesial,'[14] then fundamental theology also has a clear charter in this. It engages in opening a passageway within the Church between many interconnected realities: faith, belief and non-belief; various beliefs in comparison; worlds and cultures in dialogue; past and future in search of a meaning in Christ.

Theology is born of dialogue and the search for meaning, making comparisons.

'Our formulations of faith come from dialogue, encounter, comparison, contact with different cultures communities, nations, situations that required greater reflection when faced with what had not been made explicit earlier. Therefore, pastoral events have considerable value. And our faith formulations are an expression of an ecclesially lived and pondered life.'[15]

What, then, are the three ingredients which are indispensable for good theology according to the Pope? Study, encounter with reality, prayer.

'If study is lacking, then one can say nonsense or idealise situations in a simplistic way. If there is no real and objective context, accompanied by

---

[14] FRANCIS, *Video message of the Holy Father to the International Congress of Theology*
[15] FRANCIS, *Video message of the Holy Father to the International Congress of Theology*

those who know the environment and help, foolish idealisms can arise. If there is a lack of prayer and discernment, we can be very good sociologists or political scientists, but we will not have the evangelical audacity and the evangelical cross that we must carry, as I said at the beginning.'[16]

Theology that has no link with life and prayer is a science about God which risks becoming an ideology: a theology which has become ideology also leads to seeing the Church ideologically.

'If only the academic part is considered, there is a danger of sliding into ideologies, and this makes one sick. And it also sickens one's conception of the Church. To understand the Church, one must understand her through study but also through prayer, through community life and through apostolic life. When we slide into an ideology and go down this road, we will have a non-Christian hermeneutics, a hermeneutics of an ideological Church.'[17]

Theology becomes ideology when it is locked into particularities and no longer communicates with reality.

---

[16] FRANCIS, 'Have Courage and Prophetic Audacity' (p. 425 in the original in *La Civiltà Cattolica*, 2016).

[17] FRANCIS, *Address of the Holy Father to Rectors and students of Pontifical Colleges and Residences in Rome* (12-05-2014)

'Every attempt, every quest to reduce communication breaks the relationship between the received Tradition and concrete reality, puts the faith of the people of God at risk. Considering one of the two to be insignificant is to enter a labyrinth which will not be the bearer of life for our people. Breaking this communication easily leads to making an ideology of our view and our theology.'[18]

That the theologian may have fallen into the trap of ideology is confirmed by the marriage of his theology with casuistry. Casuistry along with ideology 'is the sign of recognising someone who knows his or her doctrine and theology off by heart but without faith. Because faith is never abstract: it needs to be witnessed to.'[19]

No 'superficial optimism' and not even a simple 'looking at things benevolently.' Much more than that it is a case of 'knowing how to correctly take risks,'[20] because it is really hope that creates a just world!

If in the past, fundamental theology was described as 'threshold theology', with Pope Francis

---

[18] FRANCIS, *Video message of the Holy Father to the International Congress of Theology*

[19] FRANCIS, Morning meditation in the chapel at the *Domus Sanctae Marthae. Faith is not casuistry* (21-02-2014)

[20] FRANCIS, *Address of the Holy Father to those taking part in the Congregation for Catholic Education Plenary Meeting* (09-02-2017).

we can risk an even stronger image: pioneer theology. Theologians are 'pioneers': 'This is important: pioneers, Onward! - Pioneers of dialogue of the Church with culture, But this being pioneers is also important because sometimes we can think they have stayed behind in the barracks ... No, at the frontier!'[21] Theology in the barracks? Certainly not. Theology on the frontier, yes, on the front line and not in the laboratory.

'There is always the lurking danger of living in a laboratory. Ours is not a "lab faith," but a "journey faith," a historical faith. God has revealed himself as history, not as a compendium of abstract truths. I am afraid of laboratories because in the laboratory you take the problems and then you bring them home to tame them, to paint them artificially, out of their context. You cannot bring home the frontier, but you have to live on the border and be audacious.'[22]

In a particular way that is true for the communication of faith, and for charity, and it is 'useful' to be able to pour 'oil and wine on the wounds of the people' we meet along the road.[23]

---

21 Francis, *Address to members of the International Theological Commission.*

22 A. Spadaro, *Interview with Pope Francis*, (21.09.2013).

23 Cf. Francis, Address of the Holy Father Francis to the academic community of the John Paul II Pontifical Institute for studies on marriage and the family (27-10-2016). On that

The description of fundamental theology is thus presented as a 'mission both fascinating and risky'[24] in a pontificate which indicates it prefers a 'key that opens' theology to a 'nail that fastens' theology.

This does not seek to be an introduction to fundamental theology. Rather is it an introduction to the meaning of this book: lecturers from the Department of Fundamental Theology in the Faculty of Theology at the Pontifical Gregorian University have assembled elements from Pope Francis' Magisterium which make up fundamental theology as a key, not a nail.

We can read the various contributions in this volume, brief and precise as they are, with profit. The group comprises nine lecturers, six of them Jesuits: Joseph Xavier (India), Ferenc Patsch (Hungary), Andrew Downing (USA), Nicolas Steeves (France), Gerard Whelan and James Corkery (Ireland), and three female lecturers: Carmen Aparicio Valls

---

occasion the Pope had reminded them of what he said on 3 March 2015. Here is the entire quote: 'Let us not forget that also good theologians, like good pastors, smell of the people and the street and, by their reflection pour oil and wine on the wounds of the people'... Theology and pastoral ministry go hand in hand.' *Ibid*, 5.

24 FRANCIS, *Address to members of the International Theological Commission.*

Introduction

(Spain), Stella Morra (Italy), Michelina Tenace (Italy), the Head of Department.

It is as Head of Department that I thank each one for having happily accepted the challenge of working, reflecting, growing together as a team within an academic institution we love and know to be, firstly, at the service of the students entrusted to us. A sincere thanks to the students, too, for supporting this vision of study as a journey of Church which is enriched from the periphery to the centre and from the centre to the periphery for the greater glory of God.

Joseph Xavier, SJ

THE DYNAMICS OF FAITH IN POPE FRANCIS' THINKING

From a biblical and Christian perspective, faith is the only way in which man is able to have a relationship with God. The Church teaches that faith, while being a divinely infused gift of God, is a genuine human act.[1] Here, faith is understood as the human response to God's revelation. While reaffirming the previous Church teachings, Vatican II states: 'The obedience of faith is to be given to God who reveals, an obedience by which man commits his whole self freely to God' (*DV* 5). The post-conciliar Magisterium continues to hold this understanding of faith. For example, according to Pope John Paul II, 'faith is said first to be an obedient response to God'.[2] In the same way, in the Post-Synodal Exhortation, *Verbum Domini* (*VD*), Pope Benedict XVI holds that faith is the proper human response to the Word of God.

---

1 Cf. *Catechism of the Catholic Church*, 153-15.
2 John Paul II, *Fides et Ratio*, 13.

Faith as human response to God's love

Pope Francis continues to reflect along the lines of his predecessors. In his first magisterial document, *Lumen Fidei* (*LF*),[3] he says, 'faith is our response to a word which engages us personally, to a "Thou" who calls us by name' (*LF* 8). Moreover, he specifies that, for him, 'faith is born from the encounter with Jesus. A personal encounter, which has touched my heart and given direction and new meaning to my existence.'[4] That is to say, for him, faith is not an abstraction or the outcome of the human search for meaning, but the consequence of God's meeting with man, i.e. the revelation of God. At the same time, one needs to remember that 'there is no God without Christ. A God without Christ,

---

[3] Pope Francis' reflection on faith in *Lumen Fidei*, as he himself reminds us, is in continuity with the traditional teachings of the Church (cf. *LF* 7, note 7). Though an encyclical of Pope Francis, it also reflects the work of his predecessor. Pope Benedict XVI had almost completed the first draft of this encyclical before he renounced the Petrine ministry. While acknowledging his indebtedness to his predecessor, Pope Francis states: 'I have taken up his fine work and added a few contributions of my own' (*LF* 7). Being a combined work, it is difficult to say where Benedict XVI ends and where Francis begins. In such a scenario, one can say that the encyclical is 'the work of four hands'. Cf. S. Ryłko, 'Una rivoluzione silenziosa', *L'Osservatore Romano*, 21 July 2013, 8.

[4] Francis, 'Parliamo della fede', *L'Osservatore Romano*, 12 September 2013, 6.

"disincarnate," is a god that is not real'.⁵ Jesus Christ is the expression of God's love towards us (Heb 1:1-2).⁶ In fact, for Pope Francis, everything begins with the premise that 'God is love' (1 Jn 4:8). While reflecting on the encyclical of his predecessor, *Deus Caritas Est*, Pope Francis outlines his understanding of this central proclamation of Christian faith:

> God does not simply have the desire or capacity to love; God is love: charity is his essence, it is his nature. He is unique, but not solitary; he cannot be alone, he cannot be closed in on himself because he is communion, he is charity; and charity by its nature is communicated and shared. In this way, God associates man to his life of love, and even if man turns away from him, God does not remain distant but goes out to meet him. This going out to meet us, culminating in the Incarnation of his Son, is his mercy. It is his way of expressing himself to us sinners, his face that looks at us and cares for us.⁷

Being love, God takes the initiative to meet us and to share his life with us in Christ. Here, God articulates his innermost reality not as an indifferent

---

5   FRANCIS, 'La bussola del credente', *L'Osservatore Romano*, 3 March 2017, 8.
6   Cf. FRANCIS, *Misericordiae Vultus*, 1.
7   FRANCIS, 'Il cuore e la bussola', *L'Osservatore Romano*, 27 February 2016, 8.

God, but as the One who is *actively* present *for* his people and *with* his people. As Kasper reminds us, God's being is Being-for-his-People; God's being as *Pro-existence* is the wonderful mystery of his essence.[8] From a Christian perspective, God is defined as the One that communicates and bestows himself as gift. As self-radiating love, the one God, at the same time, is the triune God. Only if God in himself is self-communicating love can he communicate himself externally as the one who he already is. The Incarnation is the expression of this divine love. Christians participate in this *being-for* of Christ.[9] Pope Francis confirms this understanding of Christian faith when he says, 'Christians profess their faith in God's tangible and powerful love which really does act in history and determines its final destiny: a love that can be encountered, a love fully revealed in Christ's passion, death and resurrection' (*LF* 17). This love is so decisive that it does not recoil even before death. As Ratzinger says, in the pierced heart of the Crucified, we see who God is and what he is like. Heaven is no longer locked up. God has

---

8 Cf. W. KASPER, *Misericordia: concetto fondamentale del vangelo — chiave della vita cristiana*. Brescia: Queriniana, 2013, 78.
9 Cf. J. SERVAIS, BENEDICT XVI, 'La fede non è un'idea ma la vita', *L'Osservatore Romano*, 17 March 2016, 5.

stepped out of his hiddenness.[10] The Christian faith begins precisely from that revelation of love. Simply put, the Christian faith is born of God's infinite love (*LF* 28).

Furthermore, Pope Francis insists that the Christian faith flows from the fundamental principle that God has loved us *first* (1 Jn 4:19). 'Because God is first; God is always first and makes the first move'.[11] That is to say, in the dynamics of faith, God's love has primacy. While elaborating the faith of the meek and humble, Pope Francis describes how faith emerges from God's love: 'First of all, it needs to be said that faith is God's gift to us. God continuously showers his love on us, and that makes us Christians. To say it in our local dialect Lunfardo (Buenos Aires street dialect), God always is before us, he always anticipates us (*El nos primerea*). God loves us first, seeks us out first and awaits us first.'[12] Further, this love of God has taken a concrete form: God has become man in Jesus Christ.

---

10 J. RATZINGER, *Introduzione allo spirito della liturgia*. Cinisello Balsamo (MI): San Paolo, 2001, 44.

11 A. SPADARO, 'Intervista a Papa Francesco', *L'Osservatore Romano*, 21 September, 2013, 7. This interview (Spadaro, 'Interview with Pope Francis') is available online in English, including on the Holy See's website.

12 J.M. BERGOGLIO – POPE FRANCIS, 'Prefazione' in E.C. Bianchi, *Introduzione alla teologia del popolo*, Bologna, 2015, 13-14.

When the Christian knows that the Lord has taken the initiative or the first step (*primerear*), his attitude to life changes. He becomes aware of the fact that the Holy Spirit continues to guide him in the daily events of life. It calls for constant discernment. That is to say, once a person becomes a real follower of Christ, he realises that his faith is not a fixed theory, but a praxis. Faith is an invitation to act like Christ. Faith as following of Christ prompts him to ask himself: If Jesus were in my place, what would he do? Faith thus becomes a real living of the Gospel in everyday life.

Journey of faith

One of the reoccurring themes in Pope Francis' writings and discourses is the notion of journey. For example, in his very first homily delivered the day after his election, Pope Francis speaks of 'walking' in the presence of God. In another occasion he says, 'ours is not a "lab faith," but a "journey faith".'[13] If ours is a 'journey faith' we are called to walk in the presence of the Lord like Abraham, our father in faith (Rom 4:16).[14] When Abraham is called out

---

13   A. Spadaro, 'Intervista a Papa Francesco', 8.
14   Francis, 'Non sono solo stelle', *L'Osservatore Romano*, 29 December 2016, 8.

of his homeland and sent forth as a nomad into an unknown land (Gen 12:1-3), he willingly obeys God. He believes in the promise of God, even when the evidence seems to point the other way (Gen 22:1-12).[15] Here, Abraham's obedience of faith is not a belief in some abstract truths, but his firm trust (*amen*) in God. In short, faith as walking in the presence of God consists in our willingness to let ourselves be constantly challenged, transformed and renewed by God's call (*LF* 13).

What stops people from walking in the presence of God is their inability to let themselves be guided by God. For such people, God is just a convenient idea, not a living reality that touches their everyday life. Those who lack faith hold on to the things of this world and, at times, their own ideas and ideologies, even about matters pertaining to God and religion: 'How often do we paralyse ourselves by refusing to transcend our own ideas of God, a god created in the image and likeness of man!'[16] When

---

[15] In the act of trusting God, Abraham is ready to renounce everything, even his relationship with his son. While commenting on the scene where Abraham is about to sacrifice his son Isaac, Kierkegaard visualises a soliloquy that highlights Abraham's faith: 'Lord in heaven I thank Thee; it is after all better that he believe I am a monster than that he lose faith in Thee.' S. KIERKEGAARD, *Timore e tremore*. Milan: BUR, 2001, 33.
[16] FRANCIS, 'Estremismo della carità', *L'Osservatore Romano*, 30 April, 2017, 8. Cf. SPADARO, 'Intervista a Papa Francesco', 7.

a Christian becomes a disciple of an ideology, he loses the power of faith: he is no longer a disciple of Jesus, but a disciple of a particular thought. In the same way, when the faith of the Church becomes an ideology it frightens people and it chases them away. If an individual Christian is not attentive, his faith can easily degenerate into an ideology. Based on human reasoning, he may look for clarity that leaves no room for confusion.[17]

Subtle idolatry can also hinder us from walking in the presence of God. From the Bible we know that the antithesis of faith is not atheism, but idolatry (*LF* 13). Indeed, idolatry can creep into our faith journey. When faith is reduced to a bundle of principles or seamless doctrines, it can degenerate itself into a slavish worship of rules.[18] In *Evangelii Gaudium* (*EG*) Pope Francis reminds us that such an attitude fails to see that the ultimate goal of our faith journey is *Credere in Deum*, i.e. a faith that works through love (Gal 5:6; *EG* 124). A distorted faith assumes that man is created for this world and its Sabbaths! Eventually, it gives rise to 'spiritual worldliness' (*EG* 93-97). It forgets that man is created in God's image

---

(Interview with Pope Francis).
17 Cf. FRANCIS, 'Discepoli di Cristo non dell'ideologia', *L'Osservatore Romano*, 18 October 2013, 8.
18 Though dogmas, rules and regulations are indispensable means for regulating Christian life, they cannot replace God.

with dignity and responsibility. In such cases, faith is no more a theological virtue that depends on God's grace, but a Pelagian search for self-perfection. Therefore, Pope Francis invites us to trust God even in our human failures: 'My grace is sufficient for you, for my power is made perfect in weakness' (2 Cor 12:9; *EG* 85).

People of God and the sense of faith

For Pope Francis, faith does not exist in a vacuum. Faith is alive in the community of believers. Faith is alive only when it is shared and nurtured. Therefore, faith cannot be separated from the 'faithful people' of God. That is to say, faith becomes a reality only in the life of the people. In this regard, one may notice that the thoughts of Pope Francis are influenced by 'the theology of the people' espoused by the Argentinian theologians like Lucio Gera and Rafael Tello, and the reflections of the Episcopal Conference of Latin America (CELAM).

For the theology of the people, the poor are a privileged category because they are the ones who retain the culture of a nation by holding on to the historical memory of the people. Faith feeds on and is nourished by memory.[19] Endorsing the basic principles of 'the theology of the people', Cardinal Bergoglio wrote: 'When we approach our people with the gaze of the good shepherd, when we do not come to judge but to love, we can find out that this cultural way to express the Christian faith is still present among us, especially in our poor.'[20] He is of the opinion that when we walk with the poor, we understand that they live life in a transcendental sense, beyond the huge daily difficulties. According to him, these experiences should be the framework of our theological reflections. For him, faith and culture have a symbiotic relationship. Faith always expresses itself culturally.[21] In fact, he would even say that 'our formulations of the faith are expressions of a life lived and pondered as a Church.'[22]

Even though they transcend all institutional expressions of faith, the faithful people are the ones who announce the Gospel in its entirety (*EG* 101). This idea was present in Bergoglio back in the 1980s. He wrote: 'Whenever you want to know what the Church believes, go to the Magisterium, but when

---

19 Cf. FRANCIS, 'Il fiume vivo', *L'Osservatore Romano*, 5 September 2015, 8; POPE FRANCIS, 'Il progresso della fede nella vita del sacerdote', *L'Osservatore Romano*, 3 March 2017, 4.
20 BERGOGLIO – POPE FRANCIS, 'Prefazione' 14-15.
21 BERGOGLIO – POPE FRANCIS, 'Prefazione', 18-19.
22 FRANCIS, 'Il fiume vivo', 8.

you want to know how the Church believes, go to the faithful people.'[23] For him, the faithful people are infallible 'in credendo'in – believing (*EG* 124). That is what the traditional Church teaching refers to as *sensus fidei* (sense of faith). Pope Francis describes the fundamental idea thus: 'As part of his mysterious love for humanity, God furnishes the totality of the faithful with an instinct of faith – *sensus fidei* – which helps them to discern what is truly of God» (*EG* 119). Pope Francis strongly believes that «the wisdom which the Holy Spirit'[24] gives to the faithful enables them to make discernment with regard to matters of faith.

Missionary faith

For Pope Francis, the community of believers, the Church, is not just a gathering of individuals for the sake of religious identity. Hence, he qualifies it with an important Christian component: *mission*. For him, the faithful people of God is a *missionary community* of believers, i.e. a community with the mandate to preach the Gospel to all humankind

---

[23] J.M. BERGOGLIO, *Meditaciones para religiosos*. Buenos Aires: San Miguel, 1982, 46.

[24] FRANCIS, 'Dio non si stanca di perdonare', *L'Osservatore Romano*, 18-19 March 2013, 7.

(*EG* 34). This missionary consciousness makes every Christian a responsible member of the Church.

Furthermore, the missionary consciousness of every Christian makes one take the first step (*primerear*), who does not wait for someone else to propel him/her because the Lord himself has already shown how to proceed. Besides, in sharing one's faith, a missionary heart is aware of the limitations of others. Therefore, the characteristic of the missionary community is that it is prepared to meet people where they are and accept them for what they are (1 Cor 9:22). If the mission of the Church is the salvation of the world, then, the concern of the Church cannot be of her self-preservation (*EG* 27) or her desire to cling on to past traditions and rubrics (*EG* 95), but her self-giving in the order of Jesus Christ (Phil 2:5-9). As Ratzinger reminds us, the pierced Heart of Jesus saves the world by opening itself. It saves by giving itself away. 'It invites us to step forth out of the futile attempt of self-preservation and, by joining in the task of love, by handing ourselves over to him and with him, to discover the fullness of love which alone is eternity and which alone sustains the world'.[25] This sharing of faith is possible only when the ecclesial vocation

---

25 J. Ratzinger, *Miremos al traspasado*. Rafaela: Fundación San Juan, 2007, 88.

becomes an 'outgoing' movement to the outskirts of its own territory or towards new socio-cultural settings (*EG* 30).

For Pope Francis, being faithful to Christ means being a missionary. That is real orthodoxy. Once a person becomes aware of the encounter with Christ he realizes that his faith flows from the love of God experienced as gratuitous grace. 'For if we have received the love which restores meaning to our lives, how can we fail to share that love with others?' (*EG* 8). For Pope Francis, the antithesis to faith is self-absorption: 'Whenever our interior life becomes caught up in its own interests and concerns, there is no longer room for others, no place for the poor. God's voice is no longer heard' (*EG* 2). Slowly, 'spiritual worldliness' creeps into the life of the Church. It in turn gives rise to 'the temptation to not complete the mission' that insists: 'Let's stop here; that's better!'.[26] Therefore the Pope reminds us that, though faith is always the same, 'it broadens and grows into a movement.'[27]

---

26 FRANCIS, 'Tentati dalla mondanità,' *L'Osservatore Romano*, 22 February 2017, 8.
27 FRANCIS, 'Dio delle sorprese', *L'Osservatore Romano*, 8-9 May, 2017, 8.

Faith as the light of life

Finally, Pope Francis presents the Christian faith as the light of life. He sees it as a life-transforming light that has its source in God. The Pope reminds us that for transmitting a purely doctrinal content, a book might suffice. For the Christian, that is not enough. He needs to know that what is handed down is the new light born of an encounter with the true God. Since the Christian faith is born of love, it can penetrate to the heart, to the personal core of each man and woman (*LF* 34). At the same time, it is also important to note that faith is not just one aspect of human life. In fact, it embraces the whole person and provides a future full of hope: 'The light of faith is unique, since it is capable of illuminating every aspect of human existence' (*LF* 4).

The light of faith never gets extinguished. We know that all human success and progress remain powerless in the face of the existential absurdity of death. 'The sun does not illumine all reality; its rays cannot penetrate to the shadow of death' (*LF* 1). Thus, as *Gaudium et Spes* reminds us, the fear of perpetual extinction shocks man to the core (*GS* 10). To those who have no faith, death announces their total destruction and complete departure. For the believer, it is entirely a different story. With his resurrection, Christ has freed man from death. Since the Risen Lord draws us beyond death, the Christian faith becomes the light that shines even in the shadow of death: 'To be Christian means not starting from death, but rather, from God's love for us which has defeated our most bitter enemy. God is greater than nothingness, and a lit candle is enough to overcome the darkest of nights.'[28]

Concluding reflections

The task of fundamental theology is to justify faith in today's world.[29] As Metz rightly mentions, since the time of the Enlightenment, a presumed or delegated authority often fails to accomplish this mission.[30] In fact, the Enlightenment, with its battle cry '*sapere aude*' (have the courage to use one's reason), calls for a responsible use of reason.[31] For fundamental theology, it is an opportunity to return to the 'subject' of faith.[32] Every Christian is called to share the Gospel of God's love through his own

---

28 FRANCIS, 'Il nucleo della fede', *L'Osservatore Romano*, 20 April, 2017, 8.
29 Cf. JOHN PAUL II, *Fides et Ratio*, 67.
30 J. B. METZ, *La fede nella storia e nella società: studi per una teologia fondamentale pratica*. Brescia: Queriniana, 1978, 45-48.
31 Cf. S. PIÉ-NINOT, *Tratado de teología fundamental*. Salamanca: Secretariado Trinitario, 2009, 32.
32 Cf. METZ, *La fede nella storia e nella società*, 65-85.

personal witnessing. That is to say, every believer as the subject of one's own faith has the responsibility to justify what he professes. Pope Francis has brought this aspect of faith when he highlights the role of the faithful people of God in the Church. For him, the people of God are the protagonists of their faith.[33]

Pope Francis' invitation to be 'responsible' believers also highlights the dynamic nature of Christian faith. That is to say, the sense of 'responsibility' resists every attempt to reduce faith to passivity. For a believer, the world is not an antechamber/waiting room, but an action field. He is not a passive spectator, but an active member of the 'field hospital' (Church).[34] Here, faith takes the form of 'concern' and 'charity': 'God is pleased only by a faith that is proclaimed by our lives, for the only fanaticism believers can have is that of charity!'[35] In other words, faith is an invitation to cooperate with God in the service of the Kingdom. From that perspective, for the Christian, the present is an opportunity to work for the good of others in whatever way one can. 'Faith is confessed in practice,

---

[33] Cf. FRANCIS, 'Più responsabilità per i laici', *L'Osservatore Romano*, 28-28 September 2015, 8.
[34] Cf. A. SPADARO, 'Intervista a Papa Francesco', 6. (Interview with Pope Francis).
[35] FRANCIS, 'Estremismo della carità', *L'Osservatore Romano*, 30 April, 2017, 8.

going out of itself, transcending itself in adoration and in service.'[36]

An authentic faith does not stop at what we believe (the content of faith). That is what Pope Francis means when he says, 'in the act of faith greater accent is placed on *credere in Deum* than on *credere Deum*' (*EG* 124). That is to say, faith is not static, but dynamic. If one does not move beyond the content of faith (*credere Deum*) and does not reach the reality it signifies (*credere in Deum*) faith remains incomplete. Though a «religious» act, it is not fully a 'Christian' act of faith. Aquinas reminds us that the demons too believe many truths about God. But their belief is not shaped by an affection for God and therefore it does not arrive at the real act of faith (*credere in Deum*).[37]

Growth in faith happens through encounters with the Lord during the course of our lives: 'When you did to the least of my brothers, you did it to me' (Mt 25:40). Are we able to recognize him among the needy? Therefore, Pope Francis gives importance to 'discernment of the opportune moment (*kairos*)' in the act of faith. It is precisely in discernment that one makes faith practical: 'Discernment is what

---

[36] FRANCIS, 'Il progresso della fede nella vita del sacerdote', *L'Osservatore Romano*, 3 March 2017, 4.
[37] Cf. *Summa Theologiae*, II-II. 5.2 2.

concretises faith, what makes it 'work through love' (Gal 5:6), what enables us to give credible witness.'[38] In short, for Pope Francis, the Christian faith is a gift as well as a task in *sequela Christi*, following Christ. But he cautions us: 'Faith does not merely gaze at Jesus, but sees things as Jesus himself sees them, with his own eyes: it is a participation in his way of seeing' (*LF* 18). In fact, faith makes the Christian *ad alterum*, the person for others in the order of Jesus Christ.

---

[38] FRANCIS, 'Il progresso della fede nella vita del sacerdote', *L'Osservatore Romano*, 3 March 2017, 4.

Maria Carmen Aparicio Valls

THE SIGNIFICANT WORD

> *'The Church is herself a missionary disciple; she needs to grow in her interpretation of the revealed Word and in her understanding of the truth' (EG 40).*

This sentence from *Evangelii Gaudium* provides us with the key to enter more deeply into an understanding of the Word and its significance in Pope Francis' written material.[1] What attracts our attention is the constant reminder to allow ourselves to be enlightened by the Word.[2] There are some fundamental passages along these lines: letting ourselves be taken over by the Word, entering

---

[1] Hence in approaching the Word through Pope Francis' written material, I limit myself to his main written works such as the Encyclicals *Lumen Fidei* (LF) (20-06-2013), *Laudato si'* (LS) (24-05-2015) and the Apostolic Exhortations *Evangelii Gaudium* (EG) (24-11-2013) and *Amoris Laetitia* (AL) (19-03-2016). For the topic under discussion also the Buill of Indiction of the Extraordinary Jubilee of Mercy *Misericordiae Vultus* (MV) (11-04-2015). The paragraph number is also indicated following the corresponding abbreviations for the quotes.

[2] The First chapter of the Apostolic Exhortation *Amoris Laetitia*: 'In the light of the Word' is therefore significant.

deeply into it, letting it grow and develop beyond all our predictions and mindsets (cf. *EG,* 22) and as a consequence of this, passing it on 'to make its beauty more clearly recognised and accepted by all' (*EG,* 42).[3] All this marks out a program of life in which it is necessary to position ourselves, to listen to the Word and meditate on it in silence (cf. *MV* 13; *AL* 227).

The Word, God's self-communication

The Word refers to the communication God makes of himself, and because of this it has many kinds of expression.[4] The Word is God himself and God is Father, Son and Spirit. This is fundamental to our faith: we believe in a God who is Father, Son and Spirit.

'The Father is the ultimate source of everything, the loving and self-communicating foundation of all that exists. The Son, his reflection, through whom all things were created, united himself to this earth when he was formed in the womb of Mary. The Spirit, infinite bond of love, is intimately present at

---

3 The Word is a 'companion on the journey' which points to the journey's goal (cf. FRANCIS, Ap. Exhort. *Amoris Laetitia*, 22).
4 For the various ways of using the phrase 'Word of God', and for its analogical use, see BENEDICT XVI, Post-synodal Apostolic Exhortation *Verbum Domini*, 7.

the very heart of the universe, inspiring and bringing new pathways' (*LS* 238).

Conscious that the Scriptures are the Word of God, the interpretation the Pope gives of the early chapters of the Book of Genesis from the trinitarian perspective, is important. Everything in creation is stamped with the distinctive seal of God. Therefore, the Pope states: 'For Christians, believing in one God who is trinitarian communion suggests that the Trinity has left its mark on all creation' (*LS* 239). Hence the importance of relationships with God, others, the earth (cf. *LS* 66) and with ourselves.[5]

The relationship among the divine persons is a communion of love.[6] Communion speaks to us of identity and dialogue. We are all invited to this communion, to this dialogue, however God's dialogue with each of us is not closed in on itself but opens up to dialogue with others. This is fundamental because genuine communion excludes nobody; we are all invited to live in it.

---

[5] 'Some currents of spirituality teach that desire has to be eliminated as a path to liberation from pain. Yet we believe that God loves the enjoyment felt by human beings: he created us and "richly furnishes us with everything to enjoy" (1 Tim 6:17). Let us be glad when with great love he tells us: "My son, treat yourself well... Do not deprive yourself of a happy day" (Sir 14:11-14)' (FRANCIS, Ap. Exhort. *Amoris Laetitia*, 149).

[6] Pope Francis will speak of the family as a loving reflection of the communion of love in the Trinity (cf. FRANCIS, Ap. Exhort. *Amoris Laetitia* 11; 29, 63, 71, 86 and others).

We cannot forget that our sharing in trinitarian communion is the result of God's mercy and tenderness.[7] We can say that the history of God's revelation is a manifestation of his mercy (cf. *MV* 7). Pope Francis will say that mercy 'is the bridge that connects God and man, opening our hearts to a hope of being loved forever despite our sinfulness' (*MV* 2). His wish comes from this: 'How much I desire that the year to come will be steeped in mercy, so that we can go out to every man and woman, bringing the goodness and tenderness of God!' (*MV* 5).

The Word of God is addressed to everyone (cf. *LS* 93). And not only: the Word is not given to us in an individual, private way but God has chosen to call us as a people, not a uniform people but embodied in many forms.[8] This is why confession of faith in the Triune God means opting for the other, implies recognising the dignity of every individual as the fruit of the Father's infinite love for everyone (cf. *EG* 178).

---

[7] From the outset, Pope Francis' magisterium has been characterised by mercy, but the mercy which is the manifestation of God's face. 50 years after the end of the Council, in the Bull *Misericordiae Vultus*, Francis once again reminds us that John XXIII, when he called the Council, wanted the Church to show herself to be the mother of mercy (Cf. JOHN XXIII, opening address of the Council, *Gaudet Mater Ecclesia* 11-12-1962)

[8] Among others, see FRANCIS, Ap. Exhort. *Evangelii Gaudium*, 112-118.

Christ the incarnate Word

God did not scorn making himself known in history (cf. *MV* 1) even to the extent of entering into our history. Speaking about the Word (with a capital 'W') in Pope Francis' works has a name: Jesus Christ. He is God's definitive Word, the fulfilment of his promises; he is the Word made flesh who took on our condition and in our language tells us that God is Father, Son and Spirit.

A prime characteristic of the Word is love: 'For God so loved the world that he gave his only Son' (Jn 3:16). Christ is the ultimate revelation of the Father's love, the face of the Father's mercy (cf. *MV* 1). This is why no one is excluded (cf. *MV* 12; *LS* 92). Nevertheless, not everyone has known Christ, not everyone walks with him, not everyone can hear his Word. Pope Francis offers a constant invitation to experience a personal encounter with Christ because 'it is not the same thing to have known Jesus as not to have known him, not the same thing to walk with him as to walk blindly, not the same thing to hear his word as not to know it, and not the same thing to contemplate him, to worship him, to find our peace in him, as not to. It is not the same thing to try to build the world with his Gospel as to try to do so by our own lights' (*EG* 266).

Hence the importance of renewing the personal encounter with Christ and proclaiming it happily and joyfully (cf. *EG* 3), without fear, without limits, going out to the peripheries (not only in our own area), taking the initiative ('*primereando*'), accompanying, allowing ourselves to be touched and seen. All this will see that the Church is a Church that 'goes forth'[9] in which young people are 'street preachers' (*callejeros de la fe*).[10]

The question Jesus puts to his apostles: 'But who do you say that I am?' (Mt 16:15) we can also put to ourselves. Who is Christ for me today? With a strongly Ignatian spirituality, Pope Francis constantly invites us to look at Jesus, to listen to his words, recognise him through his way of acting, look steadily at his gestures, his way of dealing with sinners, his feelings and attitudes towards the people especially those who suffer or are marginalised by society. He invites us to discover Jesus' harmony with creation.[11] Jesus reveals the Father's love

---

9   An idea which has been there from the beginning of his pontificate. See, among others, FRANCIS, Ap. Exhort. *Evangelii Gaudium*, Chap. 1.

10 'How beautiful it is to see that young people are "street preachers" (*callejeros de la fe*), joyfully bringing Jesus to every street, every town square and every corner of the earth!' (FRANCIS, Ap. Exhort. *Evangelli Gaudium*, 106).

11 To discover the realism of the Incarnation, among others the following are significant: FRANCIS, Ap. Exhort. *Evangelii*

The significant word

through his person, his gestures, and his words (cf. *MV* 1; *LS* 96-99), but in a particular way this love is revealed in the Paschal Mystery. The mystery of his death on the cross and resurrection introduces us to this extreme love which is difficult to explain. It is significant how the Pope invites us to contemplate the Crucified Christ, enter into Jesus' wounds to understand his love.[12] The resurrection tells us that the Word does not end with time; it opens us to hope and to extending communion to those who already enjoy seeing God.[13]

Experiencing the encounter with Jesus is a great gift. The exclamations we find in *Evangelii Gaudium* when the Pope is speaking of the temptations of pastoral workers are meaningful ones: Do not let missionary enthusiasm be stolen from us! Do not let the joy of evangelisation be stolen from us! Do not let hope be stolen from us! Do not let the community

---

Gaudium 265; *idem*, Ap. Exhort. *Amoris Laetitia*, 65, 144, 289; *Idem*, Encyc. *Laudato Si'* 96-100.

12 Cf. FRANCIS, Ap. Exhort. *Evangelii Gaudium*, 264-267. He will take this theme up again on several occasions, especially in homilies for the feast of St Thomas.

13 'The Bible tells us that God created us out of love and made us in such a way that our life does not end with death (Cf. Wis 3: 2-3). Saint Paul speaks to us of an encounter with Christ immediately after death; "My desire is to depart and be with Christ"'(Phil 1:23). With Christ, after death, there awaits us "what God has prepared for those who love him" (1 Cor 2:9).' (FRANCIS, Ap. Exhort. *Amoris Laetitia*, 256).

be stolen from us! Do not let the Gospel be stolen from us! Do not let the idea of fraternal love be stolen from us! Do not let missionary strength be stolen from us![14] These are all expressions which present us with the gift of the encounter with Christ and its consequences.

All of Christ's life is revelation, the Word who communicates himself and gives himself is relationship with the Father and what the Father has entrusted to us. This is why the encounter with Christ urges us to enter into a new relationship not only with Him but with everyone and everything. For 'God's Word teaches that our brothers and sisters are the prolongation of the Incarnation for each of us' (*EG* 179).

It is interesting to note how the Word of God involves us, makes witnesses of us, but for this to happen, to hear God's voice, it is necessary to leave behind our own interests, our self-absorption. This word invites us to run the risk of encounter with the other (cf. *EG* 88-92). The Pope's entire pontificate, his writings and gestures, persuades us to recognise that it is worth running the risk and that it is urgent that we do so because every individual is loved by God and brotherliness or sisterliness are not optional for

---

14 Cf. FRANCIS, Ap. Exhort. *Evangelii Gaudium*, 80, 83, 86, 92, 97, 101, 109.

the Christian. It is necessary to return to the roots of this, to the Father of us all. 'As salvation history progresses, it becomes evident that God wants to make everyone share as brothers and sisters in that one blessing which attains its fullness in Jesus, so that all may be one. The boundless love of our Father also comes to us, in Jesus, through our brothers and sisters. Faith teaches us to see that every man and woman represents a blessing for me, that the light of God's face shines on me through the faces of my brothers and sisters' (*LF* 54).

If accepting, welcoming every individual is necessary, then the choice for the least, for excluded individuals, the weakest ones, is an essential one (Cf. *LS* 49).

The Word in creation

The creative Word is a project of love where every creature is unique and has a meaning (cf. *LS* 76). We cannot separate the Word that creates from the Word that saves, in God.[15] God passes on something of himself in nature; everything in the world is a language of God's love (cf. *LS* 84): 'For

---

15 'In the Bible, the God who liberates and saves is the same God who created the universe and these two divine ways of acting are intimately and inseparably connected' (FRANCIS, Encyc. *Laudato si'*, 73).

Christians, believing in one God who is trinitarian communion suggests that the Trinity has left its mark on all creation' (*LS* 239). Pope Francis makes an appeal for theological reflection on the situation of humanity to begin with a comparison with today's context, in order to avoid words being emptied of their meaning (cf. *LS* 17).

The entire Encyclical *Laudato Si'* is a call to discover God in creation and the responsibility we have to look after it because 'the Bible has no place for a tyrannical anthropocentrism unconcerned for other creatures' (*LS* 68). Besides, looking after something in addition to not destroying it is to protect it and make it grow. It is contrary to being the 'absolute master'. Looking after things relates to the trust God places in us through his love which makes us participants in his work of creation (cf. *LS* 75). Respect and care for creation lead to recognising who God is, not occupying his space, avoiding appropriating what does not belong to us, for ourselves.

The theme of sharing in God's care and responsibility is also broadly developed in *Amoris Laetitia*, where the family is contemplated as a communion, and an image of divine communion.

Recognition of God in the works of creation, that Christ is present in creation from the beginning and that its destiny is shot through with the mystery of Christ, has important consequences for our lifestyle (cf. *LS* 228). Being aware that we share the same origin and destiny leads us to change our point of view, our attitudes to things and people (cf. *LS* 202). It requires attention to discovering the signs of God's presence in the world, and this is shown by more radical choices that look to the good of the individual and respect for that person's dignity, even in little choices or moments of attention that give a character to our daily life marked by the certainty of a definitive encounter with God:

'At the end, we will find ourselves face to face with the infinite beauty of God (cf. *I Cor* 13:12), and be able to read with admiration and happiness the mystery of the universe which with us will share in unending plenitude... Eternal life will be a shared experience of awe, in which each creature, resplendently transfigured, will take its rightful place and have something to give those poor men and women who will have been liberated once and for all' (*LS* 243).

'In the meantime, we come together to take charge of this home which has been entrusted to us, knowing that all the good which exists here will be taken up into the heavenly feast. In union with all creatures, we journey through this land seeking God

... Let us sing as we go. May our struggles and our concern for this planet never take away the joy of our hope' (*LS* 244).

The Word of creation also leads us to recognise the dignity of the individual,[16] a dignity that is the gift of the Father, and as a consequence one that does not depend on us. This is why it is important to go out to every human being, bringing God's kindness and tenderness (*MV* 50).[17]

Mary and the Word

Welcoming the Word leads us to look to Mary. Francis constantly invites us to do this. Mary, the woman who let herself be taken over by the Word and carried the Word in her womb, gives us the Word and leads us to it. She is a sure pathway for remaining in the Word.[18]

---

16 Cf. FRANCIS, Encyc. *Laudato Si'*, 65-75.
17 'If we accept that God's love is unconditional, that the Father's love cannot be bought or sold, then we will become capable of showing boundless love and forgiving others, even if they have wronged us' (FRANCIS, Ap. Exhort. *Amoris Laetitia*, 108).
18 Among other texts: FRANCIS, Encyc. *Lumen Fidei* 58-60; *Id*, Ap. Exhort. *Evangelii Gandium*, 284-288; *ID*, Encyc. *Laudato Si'*, 241-242; *ID*, Ap. Exhort. *Amoris Laetitia*, 30, 65; *ID,* Bull of Indiction for the Extraordinary Jubilee of Mercy, *Misericordiae Vultus*, 24.

Ferenc Patsch SJ

REVELATION, CONTEXT, TRUTH
THE MAGISTERIUM OF POPE FRANCIS AT A TIME OF TRANSITION

We will concern ourselves first of all in this essay with describing the situation worldwide as a 'time of transition' from the industrial to the post-industrial era (1). That said, we will identify some important characteristics of Pope Francis magisterium, the more important of which seem to be his recognition of context and historicity (the way things are said and the socio-cultural conditioning of truth, including theological truth) (2). Finally, we will develop, at least germinally, three detailed particular applications (moral theology, missiology and ecumenical theology) to show how the principles identified in his actual work of mythologising are expressed (3). The basic thesis of this essay is that Pope Francis' theology is the most adequate response to the challenges of the post-industrial era of the Church's history (4).

A time of transition: the need for a post-industrial theology

Tempora mutantur et nos mutamur in illis (times change and we change with them), said the ancients. Over the course of human history no century has elapsed without constant transformation in regard to culture and the lives of men and women. At times these transformations occur more rapidly, are more obvious and more profound than others. One sign of this is the simultaneous change in a whole series of factors characterising the entire society: the shift from rural to urban life when as a consequence, millions of people abandon their fields to dedicate themselves to city life (and then we see a shift of power among social classes); or when new inventions and technologies are born and, not least, when new sources of energy begin to 'be used' in economic production.

It is in times like these that an epic transition takes place that we can describe as a paradigm change in culture. However, individuals do not immediately become aware of what is really going on.

Today, too, we are going through an epic shift in society and culture, just as such a shift occurred seven thousand years ago in Mesopotamia with the 'Agricultural' Revolution (brought about by the invention of irrigation, writing, the chariot, money, commerce, school, the city ...) and as happened around 250 years ago in England with the Industrial Revolution (due to the arrival of the steam engine, factories, the assembly line, specialisation, industrial production, mass communication ...).

At world level there are many factors which mark and encourage the process currently underway. It is sufficient to mention first a few of them: *urbanisation* (today more than 50% of the world's population lives in the city while only 14% was urbanised at the beginning of the industrial period); *longevity* (in the space of just a few generations, the average lifespan has almost doubled); the *demographic explosion* (halfway through the 18th century Earth's population was little more than 700 million inhabitants, while today it is more than 7 billion); widespread *schooling* (currently obligatory in every country in the world at least theoretically); secularisation (on a global scale the trend has been for absolute monarchies and confessional states to shift toward becoming secular constitutional democracies); and globalisation which, together with *multimedia* (from television to internet) and scientific and *technological progress* have resulted in a true and proper revolution in mobility and digital communication. From the end of the 1960's sociological literature has usually understood these tendencies as the entry of a new stage into our society, the *post-industrial stage*.¹

Pope Francis' magisterium seems to be profoundly aware of the depth of social and cultural change and of its relevance for the Church and its theology. In his Encyclical *Laudato Si'* (2015) we read: 'We are the beneficiaries of two centuries of enormous waves of change: steam engines, railways, the telegraph, electricity, automobiles, aeroplanes, chemical industries, modern medicine, information technology and, more recently, the digital revolution, robotics, bio-technologies and nano-technologies.'² Before undertaking a sophisticated and balanced analysis of the situation and suggesting how to deal with it the Pope states: 'humanity has entered a new era' (*LS* 102).³

---

1 Cf. A. TOURAINE, *La société post-industrielle. Naissance d'une société*, Paris 1969; D BELL, *The Coming of Post-Industrial Society*, New York 1973,
2 FRANCIS, Encyc. *Laudato Si'* (24/05/2015), 102
3 FRANCIS, Encyc. *Laudato Si'* no. 102. The Apostolic Exhortation *Evangeli Gaudium* (2013) similarly speaks of an 'historical turning point' and an 'epochal change', mentioning 'scientific progress', 'technological innovation and … their rapid application to different ambits of nature and life' etc. Cf. FRANCIS, Ap, Exhort. *Evangelii Gandium* (24-11-2013), 52. It is timely to turn our gaze to the reflection the Pope develops on the 'challenges of urban culture' (*EG* 71-75) especially

Certainly, any interpretation of a breakdown of history would be completely out of place: in fact there are some constants, be they anthropological or soteriolgical such as the aspect of man as *capax Dei*, or a salvation history constantly tinged with universality. The ongoing task of the Church is to safeguard and pass on the *depositum fidei* and the Word of God which 'the Magisterium.... is not superior to..... but serves,'[4] even in a world in a constant state of flux.

Technological progress cannot be the judge of Revelation. The International Theological Commission rightly warns: 'social progress and [e.g.] the emancipation of women ... [cannot become] the decisive criteria for the interpretation of the meaning of dogmas'[5] Nevertheless, the interpretation of Revelation is never independent of the socio-historical context in which it is received. The characteristic *par excellence* of a good theology is precisely keeping a balance between the two extremes, on the one hand the extreme of

---

the 'cultural transformations' which bring about 'significant changes to our way of living' (*EG* 73). Cf. as well the analysis of the 'current situation of the family': FRANCIS, Post-synodal Ap. Exhort .*Amoris Laetitia* (19-03-2016), 32-59.

4 VATICAN COUNCIL II Dogmatic Constitution on Divine Revelation, *Dei Verbum* (18-11-1965), 10.

5 INTERNATIONAL THEOLOGICAL COMMISSION, *The interpretation of dogma*, (1990), 1.

interpreting the Holy Scripture and Tradition as if they were immutable in every detail, and, on the other, eliminating the divine truth of Revelation by depriving it of its universal and supra-cultural claims. Pope Francis' magisterium, while ably avoiding both the Scylla of rigid conservation and the Charybdis of historical relativism, focuses on the contextual aspect of truth (even revealed truth!), thus limiting in a salutary and sometimes necessary way the customary claim to universality of the Magisterium.

Re-evaluation of Context and limits as a feature of his magisterium

The opinion that one of the principal characteristics of Pope Francis' theology is the acknowledgment that theological truths never exist in the abstract in and for themselves can be defended but, following the Thomistic axiom, always and only '*ad modum recipientis*'[6] meaning when they are part of an historical, concrete context and embodied in

---

6 *Quidquid recipitus ad modum recipientis recipitur* (what is received by a person is received according to the nature of the recipient). As St Thomas states: 'Things known are in the knower according to the manner of knowing' (*cognita sunt in cognoscente secundum modum Cognoscentis*), St Thomas, *Summa Theologica* II-II q. 1, a. 2)

it. Such a discovery urges this magisterium to realise a certain 'self-limitation' of its claim to validity and this happens in a much clearer manner compared to his predecessor. Let us analyse what has been said, firstly by arguing from a philosophical and theological point of view (1); then subsequently we will see how all this shows up in Pope Francis' teaching (2); finally, which approach it requires (3).

1. Philosophical and theological considerations: the historical conditioning of magisterial statements. – All kinds of truth, including truths of faith, are subject to historical conditioning since they are formulated in a concrete linguistic manner and do not remain simply 'inner intuitions (*verbum interius*).[7] The greatest Christian theologians have always been aware of this fact, at least instinctively, and have considered it to be part of the incomprehensibility of the Mystery of God which the human being can only see imperfectly in the here and now, 'For now we see in a mirror, dimly' (1 Cor 13:12). Nevertheless, explicit awareness of this conditioned nature of truth was raised to the conceptual level, for the first time, in the modern era: this is the '*geschichtliches Bewusstein*' [historical awareness] of the Enlightenment and the German

---

7 Cf. St Augustine, *De Trinitate* 15, 11.

historical tradition (Ranke, Droysen, Dilthey).[8] Only in our days, with the birth of a philosophical hermeneutics, have these ideas matured into an adequate set of tools for speaking about it, avoiding historical relativism but restoring the logic of genuine historicity.[9] In theology, this awareness was developed, firstly, by Reformation theologians, then after some exaggerations and erroneous interpretations at a time marked by the "modernist crisis", by Catholic theologians, (J.H. Newman, B. Lonergan, K. Rahner). Finally, the very idea of the development of dogma gained full legitimacy within the context of a Catholic theological scientific approach.[10]

In fact, already for a long time a certain history of dogmatic formulation in the Catholic Church's Magisterium has been acknowledged. However, one could gain the impression that only the existence of history was admitted and once it was declared it would have achieved the absolute summit of the *insuperable* word, beyond which no one could go any

---

8 Cf. H-G. GADAMER, *Wahreit und Methode, Grundzüge einer philosophischen Hermeneutik*, Tübingen 1960, 250-290.
9 'Historical awareness ... must ... succeed in keeping in mind its own historicity.' (*die eigene Geschichtlickeit mitdenken*) (H-G. GADAMER, *Wahreit und Methode*, 366).
10 Cf. INTERNATIONAL THEOLOGICAL COMMISSION, *The interpretation of dogma* (1990).

further. In general, magisterial statements gave the impression that the concepts employed in dogmatic formulation were clear, univocal and accessible to anyone's understanding. It seemed to be the same principle as a mathematical truth where 2+2=4 and any further clarification was neither necessary nor possible. Instead, some theologians have recently reflected on the matter, arguing how such a theory is inadequate given that some of the assumptions are in themselves problematic. Indeed, as Karl Rahner correctly notes, the transmission of Divine Revelation immediately encounters important difficulties as soon as it enters an historical situation:[11] even dogmatic formulations of the Magisterium are conditioned by concepts that come under the influence of language and the general circumstances of a determined cultural period. The Church's Magisterium is not able to and in principle cannot establish the desirable ('perennial') concepts for its formulations on its own, autocratically. Linguistic development also takes place independently from this Magisterium.

Although the 'regulation of language' (*spachraegelung*) may be a right and duty of its

---

[11] Cf. K. RAHNER, "Mysterium Ecclesiae": *Zur Erklärung dei Glaubenskongregation über die Lehre der Kirche* in ID., Schriften zus Theologie, Vol. 12, Zürich 1975, 482-500.

supreme and universal holder, he cannot delude himself by thinking it is possible to formulate *the* Revelation once and for all: it will always be necessary to reformulate it or, at least, reformulate some of its truths by using other language, less imperfect, more comprehensible for someone who lives in another context and at another time, by inserting it into the broader context of other truths of faith, Revelation is at least in some ways reformable: it can be expressed more completely, more relevantly, thus making its reception or its response to the new questions of the time simpler, ensuring that the truth of the faith stands out when confronted with the new errors that arise. After this philosophical and theological analysis of the concept of Revelation as the historically conditioned truth of faith, we will now look for signs of this idea in Pope Francis' Magisterium.

2. A novelty of Pope Francis' magisterium: 'awareness of its own limitations' (LS 105) – One of the features of Pope Francis' magisterium is the courage with which he expresses the historical and cultural context of theology in general and his own magisterium in particular. This can be clearly seen in certain passages of his Apostolic Exhortation *Evangelii Gaudium* (2013). Already at the beginning of the text when proposing a 'sound decentralisation' in practice, the Pope reflects on the limits of his own initiative: 'Nor do I believe that the papal magisterium should be expected to offer a definitive or complete word on every question which affects the Church and the world. It is not advisable for the Pope to take the place of local Bishops in the discernment of every issue which arises in their territory' (*EG* 16). The idea returns later when the Pope confirms that 'neither the Pope nor the Church have a monopoly on the interpretation of social realities or the proposal of solutions to contemporary problems' (*EG* 184), and referring to Pope Paul VI he adds: 'In the face of such widely varying situations, it is difficult for us to utter a unified message and to put forward a solution which has universal validity. This is not our ambition, nor is it our mission. It is up to the Christian communities to analyse with objectivity the situation which is proper to their own country.'[12]

The notion of self-limitation, evident since his election, is not completely new. More than being an absolute novelty, in the case of Francis' magisterium we are dealing with a more marked emphasis and maybe also a variation in his spiritual attitude. However, what we can marvel at is the frequency of

---

12 FRANCIS, Ap. Exhort. *Evangelii Gaudium*, 184. Cf. PAUL VI, Ap Lett. *Octogesima Adveniens*, (14-05-1971), 4.

this theme. 'In her dialogue with the State and with society, the Church does not have solutions for every particular issue' (*EG* 241) – and in the previously cited Encyclical *Laudato Si'* (2015) on the ecology, the Pope criticizes the attitude of those who forget their own limitations: 'Each age tends to have only a meagre awareness of its own limitations' (*LS* 105). We are certainly not dealing with a weakening of the truth of Revelation on the part of the Magisterium. On the contrary: to carry out the Pope's program and, following in the wake of John Paul II and Paul VI, to build a 'culture of life' and a 'civilisation of love' (*LS* 231) based on the Gospel, Francis maintains that it is necessary for those worldwide who support this to learn '[the] limits that a healthy, mature and sovereign society must impose' (*LS* 177) and, no less, that the Church's Magisterium itself develop a new post-industrial spirituality sensitive to the other and the other's context. This undertaking certainly cannot be realised without a degree of self-limitation.

Finally, also the vision of the post-synodal Apostolic Exhortation *Amoris Laetitia* (2016), by foregrounding the importance of discernment as an essential aspect of moral decision-making, places a focus on the conditioned and contextualised aspect of revealed truth, emphasising our limitations in reference to the possibility of knowing about it only according to 'different states of growth' (*AL* 295; Cf. 300; 303; 312). Put succinctly, one of the main features of Pope Francis' magisterium is the willingness to understand the consequences of theology's contextuality, keeping its historical, cultural and linguistic conditions in mind, and recognising the effect of these on the interpretation of Church teaching, including magisterial teaching. Now we need to identify the necessary approach for obtaining this specific goal.

3. Inductive method – One feature, if indeed not a specific difference of Pope Francis' magisterium, is hidden within his method or approach. The approach most often used by pontiffs prior to him has been the *deductive method*, or the *modus procedendi* which the holders of supreme and universal power in the Church have habitually employed. There are few exceptions to this trend, amongst which is *Gaudium et Spes* (1965), the Pastoral Constitution of Vatican II, whose formulators chose *not* to proceed according to the classic dogmatic approach of neo-scholasticism. They chose not to start out from scriptural, patristic, dogmatic statements understood as general principles, to ultimately arrive at their application to today's concrete situations. Instead they went the other way.

By starting from below, so to speak, Pope Francis has gone back to this alternative tradition, wanting to continue the approach begun by the Council. The method developed in Francis' magisterium takes concrete historical reality as its point of departure, in order to read 'the signs of the times' in it and seek a Christian solution to the matters in question through theological reflection in the light of Revelation and Tradition. Let us look at some examples of how this approach functions and where it leads to.

An 'incarnated' magisterium: three examples

One of the main specifics of Pope Francis' theology is his recognition of the fact that theology (including magisterial theology) and context (socio-cultural) are inseparably interlinked. Hence the question arises: 'Which theology is desirable in a post-industrial context? How does the self-limitation of Francis' magisterium function in practice?' We will look now at the consequences of the principles mentioned earlier in three different specific fields (1. Moral Theology: 2. Missiology: 3. Ecumenical Theology). Certainly, given the complexity and richness of the theme, we can only offer some essential references.

1. Moral theology for the formation of Consciences (Cf. AL 37) – It is not necessary to be experts in the social sciences to be able to observe the fact that in the emerging post-industrial society the situation of the family has changed radically. When marriage was the result of an agreement between two families and supported with all the strength of the entire society ('social control') it was difficult for a couple to find themselves in a crisis of identity, and divorce was practically non-existent.

Beginning with the industrial stage of global culture, the situation gradually began to change. In 1930 Pope Pius XI was still speaking of the 'right ordering' of the family, which required 'both the primacy of the husband with regard to the wife and children, the ready subjection of the wife and her willing obedience.'[13] Today instead, in the light of popular psychology, for most theologians these words of the Pontiff are seen out of date (if not downright antiquated and unacceptable).

In its time, *Gaudium et Spes* (1965) opened a new chapter, dealing with the purpose and dignity of marriage and the family from a more existential and personalist point of view (*GS* 47-52). The Council Fathers did mention divorce but only marginally,

---

13 Pius XI, Encyc. on Christian marriage, *Casti Connubii* (31-12-1930), 31.

stigmatising it as an 'epidemic' (*GS* 47). But the Constitution said nothing about themes which are so central today, such as couples living together before marriage, or the possibility of Eucharistic Communion for divorced Catholics living in a second Civil marriage.[14]

Today, more than half a century after the closure of the Council, more than half the marriages in the Western World end in divorce. This is also the case in the United States, where the percentage of divorce, including among Catholics, has risen to 40%. In large cities the majority of couples live together (this is also happening among those who wish to be married in Church).

Tackling this situation, Pope Francis, in *Amoris Laetitia* (2016), demonstrated great realism and an eminently pastoral attitude. With the wealth of experience of two Synods of Bishops behind him in 2014 and 2015, he begins from the concrete experience of people in their socio-cultural context.

Recognising the existing difficulties, the post-synodal Apostolic Exhortation presented a positive and confident theological perspective in reference to 'love in the family', showing the beauty of married and family life. After some wise, practical and

---

14 G. O'COLLINS, 'Pope Francis and the Second Vatican Council', *The Pastoral Review* (January/February 2017) 6-9.

profound advice with which the Pope intended to strengthen the relationships of couples and family members along the lines of personal development, in Chapter 8 entitled 'Accompanying, discerning and integrating weakness' (*AL* 291-312) the document seeks to tackle compassionately the situation, too, of those who live in 'various so-called 'irregular' situations' (*AL* 296-300).

While maintaining the *depositum fidei,* that is, while safeguarding the indissolubility of marriage, which Christ himself wanted (*AL* 62), Pope Francis introduces a new disciplinary regulation (note, not a doctrinal one!) concerning the possibility of admitting divorced and remarried people to Eucharistic Communion 'in certain cases' (*AL* 305, note 351) after an essential personal and pastoral discernment (*AL* 79; 299; 304) and no longer demanding commitment to sexual continence in every case, still requested by *Familiaris Consortio* (1981) by John Paul II (*FC* 84). With this new practice, undoubtedly, the role of the priest and confessor has become much more demanding and responsible.

This leads to the theological re-evaluation of the central place of conscience in moral behaviour.[15]

---

15 Cf. C. GRECO, 'Caratteristiche, valore teologico e recezione di Amoris Laetitia' *Rassegna di tealogia* 54/4 (2016) 533-557.

In this regard the Pope writes: 'Recognising the influence of such concrete factors, we can add that individual needs to be better incorporated into the Church's praxis in certain situations which do not objectively embody our understanding of marriage' (*AL* 303).

And elsewhere, we read a concluding appeal which seems to be fully in harmony with the state of mind of a mature Christian of our time: 'We have been called to form consciences, not to replace them' (*AL* 37). One can discuss whether such a self-definition, contextually sensitive, of the role of the Magisterium is truly self-limiting and in what sense, or whether instead it might be the expression of an even more worthy and ambitious enterprise than what came before.

2. Missiology, the paradigm for all theology for all theology (Cf EG 15) – In the context of the post-industrial world, no less evident is the change regarding the situation of the missions. While modern western civilisation remained convinced of its superiority, everyone took the strict co-operation between missionaries and Colonial Powers for granted. But when the political system of colonialism collapsed ('the second decolonisation': 1945-1999) the theology of mission became aware of the fact that there are other interpretations of the history of salvation than a European one. With the end of modernity's 'grand narratives', missiology too made way for other, alternative interpretations ('post-colonial theology'). Naturally, the central place of Jesus Christ was never in doubt (Cf *DI*). However it would be unrealistic to think that the drastic changes in the historical and socio-cultural context of humanity could leave intact the theological interpretation of the eternal destiny of individuals living in a determined context. Missiology (as also the theology of the history of salvation and of religions) was destined for further development.

The watershed in this case, too, was the Second Vatican Council. In a brief but rich decree on the Church's missionary activity, *Ad Gentes* (1965), the Council Fathers considered missionary activity not as something secondary, but as a real part of the nature of the Church itself and, as a consequence, a constituent part of its most intimate identity! 'The pilgrim Church is missionary by her very nature' (*AG* 2). Thus, the way was open for Western culture to be separate from the Catholic Church (*GS* 42) which gradually made it possible to surmount the '*plantatio ecclesiae*' paradigm which in practical terms had not yet recognised inculturation.

But the real new horizons in missiology opened with the pontificate of Pope Francis. From his first appearance he presented himself as a missionary Pope *par excellence* and his magisterium also reflects this.

The Apostolic Exhortation *Evangelii Gaudium,* whose first chapter is entitled 'The missionary transformation of the Church" (*EG* 19-49), is an entire joyful and refreshing source with much to say about the proclamation of the gospel, today's world, and to Christians understood as missionaries.[16]

This lengthy text, which takes up many of the themes in *Redemptoris Missio* (1990) by John Paul II and other themes from Pope Benedict XVI, was conceived around the time 'new evangelisation'[17] came on the scene (cf. *EG* 120), but Pope Francis goes beyond their formulation, emphasising that 'all the baptised, whatever their position in the Church.... Are agents of evangelisation' (*EG* 120). Lengthy intellectual preparation and many lessons in theology are not necessary. What counts is experience of God's love: 'Every Christian is a missionary to the extent that he or she has encountered the love of

---

[16] Cf. S. B. BEVANS, 'The Apostolic Exhortation *Evangelii Gaudium* on the Proclamation of the Gospel in Today's World', *International Review of Mission* 10 3/2 (2014) 297-308.

[17] We need to remember that in 2012 an entire Synod was dedicate to the topic of 'new evangelisation'. The title of the *Instrumentum Laboris* was 'New Evangelisation for the Transmission of the Christian Faith'.

God in Christ Jesus' (*EG* 120). So the best formation for evangelisation is ' deepening love' (*EG* 121).

In the field of mission, Francis makes room for great diversity nourished by 'pastoral creativity' (*EG* 145) and 'missionary creativity' (*EG* 25; cf. *EG* 156). In fact 'we should not think, however, that the Gospel message must always be communicated by fixed formulations learned by heart or by specific words which express an absolutely invariable content' (*EG* 129). Beginning with the 'transcultural' nature of the Gospel (*EG* 117), a process of 'inculturation is inevitable' (*EG* 116; 120; 122; 126, 129; and also implicitly, 118; 121),[18] a process also advanced through dialogue (*EG* 238). Herewith the concluding wish of the Pope regarding the missions: 'I dream of a "missionary option", that is, a missionary impulse capable of transforming everything, so that the Church's customs, ways of doing things, times and schedules, language and structures can be suitably channelled for the evangelisation of today's world rather than for her self-preservation' (*EG* 27). We cannot but transform the Church to be there at the cutting edge of the mission and evangelisation.

---

18 'Cultures differ much among themselves and every general principle – as I have said, dogmatic issues well-defined by the Church's magisterium – need to be inculturated if they wish to be observed and applied' (FRANCIS, Address at conclusion of 14th Ordinary Assembly of the Synod of Bishops [24-10-2015].

This enterprise presumes the respectful attention of the cultural context (post-industrial), which is a radically pluralistic one, and it opens up new directions in missiology (mission *inter gentes*; mission from the margins …)[19]

3. Ecumenical theology, a mutual (though asymmetrical) exchange (cf. EG 246) – As long as European nations were fighting religious wars (until the 16th century) the idea still seemed completely plausible that the faith of enemy countries was fundamentally in error and heretical, and could not lead to salvation. Instead, as a consequence of the Second World War, when the peoples of Europe began to mix, and different peoples entered into relationships with one another, the belief was strengthened that not even followers of another denomination were of the devil. This discovery gave birth to the ecumenical movement. Although anachronistic, we can try asking ourselves: would it not have been possible, perhaps, to avoid four centuries of murderous controversy which

---

19 For more extensive studies cf. G. COLZANI, 'Mission and Church', in F. MERONI, ed., *Mission makes the Church*, Canterano (RM) 2017, 61-126, especially 122-126; S. W. SUNQUIST 'A Historian's Hunches. Eight Future Trends in Mission', in C. E. VAN ENGEN, ed., T*he State of Missiology Today. Global Innovations in Christian Witness*, Downers Grove (Illinois)) 2016, 285-297.

characterised the relationships between Catholics and Protestants after the Reformation, if the Pope had recognised the two principal truths of the Reformers: (1) the Bible is not only important but the inevitable nourishment for the spiritual life (including of the laity!) and (2) secular wealth is a temptation, risk and trap for the Church? One thing is certain; it is not possible to achieve recognition on the basis of the old paradigm and even less to achieve unity among Christians. Is there an alternative?

In the wake of Vatican II's Decree *Unitatis Redintegratio* (1965) on ecumenism, Pope Francis has succeeded in giving new impetus to the ecumenical movement. Already from the *loggia*, the balcony of St Peter's, on his first appearance, Pope Bergoglio attracted the attention of non-Catholic Christians, especially the sister Churches of Orthodoxy, by using the self-limiting title 'Bishop of Rome'. Just as significant was the presence of the Ecumenical Patriarch of Constantinople, Bartholomeus, at the inaugural liturgy for Pope Francis' Petrine ministry – something which had no precedence. [20]It is not by chance that the name of the same Patriarch along

---

20 Cf. E. BIANCHI, 'I Quattro anni di Papa Francesco', *La Rivista del Clero Italiano* 98 (04-04-2017) 246-258, here: 252-253; G. O'COLLINS, *Living Vatican II: The 21st Council for the 21st Century*, Mahwah 2006, 29-33; 109-124.

with the then Archbishop of Canterbury, Rowan Williams, can be found in the section of *Evangelii Gaudium* dedicated to ecumenism. *(EG* 245).

'How many important things unite us! If we really believe in the abundantly free working of the Holy Spirit, we can learn so much from one another!' (*EG* 246). These are the passionate words which best express the Pope's attitude toward those whom the Council called 'separated brethren' (cf. *UR* 1). Francis prefers to describe them as those 'on pilgrimage with us.' Here we discover something new: for the Pope 'it is not just about being better informed about others, but rather about reaping what the spirit has sown in them, which is also meant to be a gift for us. To give but one example, in the dialogue with our Orthodox brothers and sisters, we Catholics have the opportunity to learn more about the meeting of episcopal collegiality, and their experience of synodality' (*EG* 246).

This mutuality of exchange, an extremely fertile (and also courageous) idea is central in Francis and emerges in various contexts: concerning inculturation,[21] the spirituality of proclaiming

---

21 According to Pope Francis it is an opportunity for us Christians 'to allow others to evangelize us' (*EG* 121).

the Gospel,[22] social work[23] and inter-religious dialogue.[24] Ecumenism is tied to all these fields. However its urgency and principal motive rely on the credibility of Christians (cf. *EG* 244) and is destined to eliminate the scandalous 'counter-witness of division among Christians' (*EG* 246)[25]

Pope Francis' gestures along this long journey with other Christians have been as significant if not more so than his words. After the meeting with the Patriarch of Constantinople and the Orthodox Archbishop of Athens, Francis described it iconically as the ecumenism of charity which can absolutely not be rejected. When he visited Turin, he wanted to meet the representatives of the Waldensians to heal, if possible, the wounds of long persecution in

---

[22] 'This message has to be shared humbly as a testimony on the part of one who is always willing to learn ...' (*EG* 128).

[23] 'We need to let ourselves be evangelised by them [the poor]' (*EG* 198).

[24] "Evangelisation and inter-religious dialogue, far from being opposed, mutually support and nourish one another' (*EG* 251). And again: 'As Christians we can also benefit from these treasures built up over many centuries, which can help us better to live our own beliefs.' (*EG* 254).

[25] In other contexts, the problem of ecumenism is not typical: in *Laudato Si'* there is positive mention of the 'same concern' shared by the Catholic Church and the other Churches and Christian Communities (cf. *LS* 7-9), besides the beauty of the 'spirituality of the Christian East' (cf. *LS* 235): *Amoris Laetitia* repeats only the teaching of J. PAUL II on problems relating to mixed marriages (cf. *AL* 247).

Italy, while at Caserta he visited a small Pentecostal group who are even more marginal in Italy, but whose pastor was a personal acquaintance of the then Archbishop Bergoglio. Then Cuba became an unforeseen and unplanned stopover, due to Pope Francis' doggedness in wanting to meet fraternally with the Patriarch of Moscow, Kiril. Elsewhere too, in Georgia, for example, he showed that he accepted and wanted to surmount the non-reciprocity of ecclesial welcome in liturgy and prayer. Finally, we should mention the Swedish city of Lund, where the Pope wanted to be present as a guest to remember, along with the Protestant Churches, the five hundred years since the Reformation; not to celebrate, as he had the opportunity to clarify, and even less to celebrate the breakdown in ecclesial communion, but rather to acknowledge how there were evangelical intentions even in Luther's initial gestures and how the break involved shared responsibility also to be laid at the feet of the Roman Church, insensitive to repeated demands for reform.[26]

By way of conclusion

What is the special feature, then, of Pope Francis' magisterium? The underlying thesis he

---

26 Cf. E. BIANCHI, 'I quattro anni di Papa Francesco', *La Rivista del Clero Italiano* 98 (04-04-2017), 246-258.

invites us to refer to is that 'Christian doctrine is not a closed system incapable of generating questions, doubts, being questioned, but is alive, knows how to disturb and animate. It does not present a rigid face, has a body that moves and develops, has a tender flesh: Christian doctrine is called Jesus Christ'.[27] Perhaps some people dream of a logically coherent doctrine which is monolithic and defended by everyone, without nuance. But such a definition of Revelation would be a real loss and weakening. For Pope Francis, 'in fact such variety serves to bring out and develop different facets of the inexhaustible riches of the Gospel' (*EG* 40).

Is it an absolutely new thing to describe Pope Francis' magisterium in these terms? We share the opinion of Italian theologian Severino Dianich that it would be incorrect to think this way. Indeed it is fundamentally mistaken to believe that by comparison with tradition Vatican II's theological shift in its view of Revelation, the replacing of the classical language of Scholasticism with a more immediate and existential language, and some of the new forms of Pope Francis' magisterium are a complete novelty. In the light of what has been said here, it seems to be clear by now that 'The tradition

---

27 Francis, Meeting with representatives of the 5th National Convention of the Italian Church (10-11-2015).

of the Faith is in fact a living tradition, one for which the Magisterium which gathers, expounds and protects it in all its authenticity has, throughout history changed its forms,'[28]

As an integral part of these dramatic 'cultural and anthropological changes' (*AL* 32) we are living at a *time of transition* – this is the statement we started out from. The conclusion of this research can be put succinctly: the theology of Pope Francis' magisterium not only has the special character of updating the Church but, by taking the initiative, of also leading us to a theology and Christian common practice which is appropriate for our post-industrial era.

---

28 S. Dianich, *Magistero in movimento. Il caso Papa Francesco*, Bologna 2016, 33.

Stella Morra

A FAITHFUL PEOPLE AMONG PEOPLES! ELEMENTS OF FUNDAMENTAL ECCLESIOLOGY

The attempt to reconstruct the underlying theology underlying the work and texts of a pastor is a very complex task, especially when the pastor in question is the Bishop of Rome, who happens to still be active (hence evolving), and when the task is to be achieved within the brief space of a few pages. An even greater difficulty lies in yet another problem! *This* pastor is characterised by the creative and productive reception of a principle espoused by the Second Vatican Council – *the pastoral nature of doctrine.*[1]

This category alters the way we understand, employ and express any theology, let alone the paradigm involving the relationship between critical thought, linguistic expression, gestures and choices, and pastoral ministry. Anyone wishing to study and understand the underlying theology, then, should

---

[1] For this theme see C. Theobald, *La recezione del Concilio Vaticano II. 1. Tornare alla sorgente*, Bologna 2011.

not give up on the task (for critical re-examination is indeed an essential step in a renewed paradigm), but should be prepared to review his or her criteria and sources out of respect for the way this theology manifests itself.

In particular, there are two pivotal issues which especially need to be borne in mind; assuming historicity to be confirmation (based on the theological principle that the history of salvation means that God continues to speak and act in history), and the circular (no longer deductive) logic of the relationship between the life of belief and its critical and linguistic know-how, a relationship which is necessary but does not mean the one is the source of the other (for the primacy of salvation over knowledge suffers when Christianity turns into gnosticism).[2]

By employing features of fundamental ecclesiology, then, we will attempt to proceed by way of roughly concentric circles to build up areas for understanding and testing more extensive studies.

---

[2] Obviously there are many risks possible: confusing '*verificazione*' or confirmation, with '*verifica*' or checking if something is true; undervaluing the role of critical thought or verbal statement. But in our opinion the directions are rather clear. (Cf. FRANCIS, Ap, Exhort. *Evangelii Gaudium* (24-11-2013), 93-97 (Henceforth *EG*).

'The People' as a point of view; life at the centre

For Pope Francis, the People of God understood as subject[3] is much more than the benevolent recognition of one subject's involvement by another, more powerful subject. Instead, it is assuming a necessary viewpoint, an indispensable one for rethinking and interpreting the Church's very own experience.

'To evoke the faithful Holy People of God is to evoke the horizon to which we are called *to look and reflect*. It is the faithful Holy People of God to whom as pastors we are continually called to look, protect, accompany, support and serve ... The pastor is pastor of a people, and *he serves this people from within* ... Looking at the People of God is remembering that we all enter the Church *as lay people* ... It does us good to remember that the Church is not an elite of priests, of consecrated men, of bishops, but that everyone forms the faithful Holy People of God. To forget this carries many risks and distortions in our own experience, be they personal or communal, of the ministry that the Church has entrusted to us.'[4]

---

3 Cf. VATICAN II Dogmatic Constitution *Lumen Gentium* (21/11/1961), 9-12; 30-31.
4 FRANCIS, *Letter to Cardinal Marc Ouellet, President of the Pontifical Commission for Latin America* (19 March 2016) (italics ours).

This understanding of the People of God as subject, already announced from his first greeting on the day of his election,[5] must not be interpreted in ordinary media terms: a gesture like that is not improvised; rather it is deeply rooted in the logic of the Council, not just at an intellectual or academic level but it has become pastoral practice, a style of personal encounter and choices for governing the Churches, as well as a place for comparison and assessment. It is so much a part of him that we should call it 'bodily' to the extent that it is gesture (not just speech), prayer and blessing (and not just teaching).

Behind the elaboration of this practice and his reflection on the privilege of the People of God as a point of view, lies not only the long history of CELAM and its Plenary Assemblies at Medellín

---

5 'And now let us begin this journey, the Bishop and people, this journey of the Church of Rome, which presides in charity over all the Churches, a journey of brotherhood in love, of mutual trust. Let us always pray for one another. Let us pray for the whole world that there might be a great sense of brotherhood … And now I would like to give the blessing, but first I want to ask you a favor. Before the bishop blesses the people, I ask that you would pray to the Lord to bless me — the prayer of the people for their Bishop. Let us say this prayer — your prayer for me — in silence.' These words were followed by the gesture of bowing and by an impressive silence in the packed square. (accessed 04/07/2017) http://vaticaninsider.lastampa.it/fileadmin/user_upload/File_Version_originale/il-primo-discorso-di-Francesco.pdf .

(1968), Puebla (1979), Santo Domingo (1992) and Aparecida (2007), but also the history of people and churches marked by the wounds of dictatorship, and poverty, theologies of liberation, the living experience of basic communities. Without this twin history we can understand precious little about how and why Pope Francis uses the category of the People of God as a key,[6] even when he is not explicitly talking about it.

This history demonstrates that the shift in point of view has a crucial first effect: to put life as it is back at the centre;[7] not 'religious' life as such but life with it's own loci and dynamics: birth, growth, looking after and consoling or being looked after and consoled, death … The People of God are a people made up of those who bless and who live from mercy and its works.

From citizens to people: an ongoing reform

The second effect of the shift in point of view is the responsibility it establishes: by definition, a

---

6 Cf. J. C. SCANNONE, "Papa Francesco e la teologia del popolo", in *La Civiltà Cattolica*. Quaderno 3930 (2014/1) 571-596.

7 FRANCIS, *Letter to Cardinal Marc Ouellet, President of the Pontifical Commission for Latin America* (19 March 2016): 'Looking to the faithful Holy People of God, and feeling ourselves an integral part of the same, places us in life and thus in the themes that we treat, *in a different way.*'

people is made up of many ages, life stories, but also roles and services. The 'experience of being a people' is only realised if each individual takes up (to the best of his or her possibilities) the responsibilities he or she has and which contributes to the common good.

This idea was clearly explained by the then Cardinal Bergoglio in a lecture he gave in 2010[8] when he noted a tension between the 'simple' understanding of humanity as made up of individuals who are the subject of rights and dignity, and the more complex understanding of humanity as beings in relationship. The dignity of the former is necessary (but not sufficient) for the latter, but while the former is made up of citizens (which is no small thing) only the latter make a unity of people, a whole made up of citizens. The notion of the common good, for example, holds up only to the extent that the understanding of self and one's rights fits in not only with a reflective view of others as subjects with rights but also with an understanding of the inevitable and complex bond which ties every self to all the others.

---

8 Cf. J. BERGOGLIO, "Nos como ciudadanos nosotros como pueblo." Conference given by the archbishop for the 13th Archdiocesan Day of Social Pastoral Ministry (16-10-2010) [accessed: 14/07/2017] http://www.arzbaires.org.ar/inicio/homilias/homilias2010.htm

The experience of this 'we', if it is not to be simply a spontaneous and somewhat theoretical desire, requires government of the process that leads inhabitants of the same territory to become citizens and then, gradually, a people who maintain their diversity in a multi-faceted harmony by recognising what they are prepared to sacrifice and what quality of relationships they need to maintain in common.

With this understanding, then, before dealing with moral topics, what is needed for civil life and the dimensions of what we call social existence are mutual trust, clear rules for living in common, and no corruption.

During the lecture mentioned above, the then Cardinal Bergoglio offered some criteria which re-appears in *Evangelii Gaudium* 217-237; these are criteria for governing and to bring about consensus: time is superior to space, unity prevails over conflict, realities are more important than ideas, the whole is superior to the part.

These criteria apply to a person understood as a relational being; they are not just wishful thinking of a spiritual or inward kind: they call for a project of co-existence and offer an idea of what a people is called to be among the peoples.

From this structure and basic set of requirements, the Church as a people, and not just any people but a People *of God*, is not only not exempt from being a prophetic sign but is indeed called to be such (a quasi-sacrament) in a process of ongoing reform.

In fact it is a matter of always finding the right form to allow and to express a liveable and visible place of tension between the possibility of the divine plan of universal salvation for the world and its inhabitants, and the life circumstances of the world throughout history which already contains this plan and is also an articulation of freedom.

The great temptation of clericalism,[9] the insistence on the centrality of processes,[10] the request to reposition our pastoral outlook[11] right down to the smallest detail[12] – all this seems to indicate, along with other emphases, how the Church's *form* and therefore it's *reform* is not an ideological issue (the tiresome debate over continuity/break from it!) but rather taking note of a period of major transition which requires that we take on a different form in order to be faithful.

---

9 Cf. Francis, *Meeting with the bishops responsible for the Latin American Episcopal Council*, (28-07-2013), 43
10 Cf. *EG* 69, 82, 129, 169-173, 223-225. Cf. also Francis, Encyc. *Lumen Fidei* (29-06-2013), 57.
11 Cf. *EG* 52-109.
12 Cf. S. Dianich, *La Chiesa Cattolica verso la sua riforma*, Brescia 2014, 140-141, on the Santa Marta Chapel as a particular style of magisterium.

According to the Council's viewpoint, the mystery of the Church is a place of tension between that which has been entrusted (nature) and received by the People of God then passed on down the ages (Scripture and Tradition), and the ongoing appeal to recognize that God is already present (mission)[13] in a history in which he continues to speak and work for the salvation of all.

This way of presenting things allows us to overcome the *ad intra /ad extra* polarised logic with regard to the Christian community and thus bring to fulfilment the centrality of life as it is. This is about work to be carried out for theological reasons, not sociological and cultural ones, by preference. This is a real venture of faith, because the gospel, as always, precedes us, and all of us, the Church first of all, are its servants and disciples.

Grace supposes culture: A faithful people among peoples

The category of culture, then, becomes decisive: culture – the public and historical name for the

---

[13] Cf FRANCIS, *Dio nella città*, Cinisello Balsamo (MI) 2013; CELAM Concluding Document of the 5th General Conference of the Latin American and Caribbean Bishops, 12 [accessed 14/07/2012], https://docs.google.com/document/d/11-DY_7A0ESB8zeSprBJUIJPld_egkhqwpbRwuO-63x2M/p2eview?pli=1

relationship between individuals which allows them to recognise themselves as 'we', a plural person. The sharing of culture is what *makes* a people, so long as culture means that composite of being and saying, gestures and names, conditions and consequences, doing and knowing, which make up the profound practical know-how of our being in the world.

Culture functions like the body does: we are in the world because we are immersed in it, cannot escape it, but we cannot make it an absolute. To encounter others, in their body, we have to 'lean out' from our own. We have to learn to say 'I' while experiencing the fact that this 'I' is already in itself, in its bodily experience, a whole which is open to what is outside it, in other words, relationship.

This is culture, then, in a plurality made up of everyone and which is inclusive of everyone; which has its logic and times and which asks for humility and respect, to be accepted before being learned, recognised and constructed, is the "flesh" of a people that recognises itself and makes room for encountering other cultures.

Again in *Evangelii Gaudium*, at the end of no. 115, we find the brief sentence that allows us to add the qualifier 'of God' to 'the people' that the Church is: 'grace supposes culture'. Grace is the ancient name for God's relationship with his people.

For centuries theology taught that 'grace supposes nature'[14] as a way of saying that the relationship God wishes to establish with men and women in time, is one according to our measure. God supposes, meaning he considers the way he has made us to be a prerequisite: we are creatures. He does not cancel out this factor nor does he ask us to deny it in order to encounter him, and he does not pose conditions which would be impossible for us or be contrary to who we are.

Pope Francis alters the sentence to preserve its deeper meaning and says that 'grace supposes culture': to become and be the People of God in history is not an alternative to being a living part of one of the peoples inhabiting history, but rather it is being, among all peoples, a people with a twofold 'we' which makes the fact visible and open to experience that there is no culture which cannot be visited and loved by the God who took flesh, and who does not cease to exist through the bodies of all men and women, especially the poor. It goes further, because every culture and every people is necessary for the flesh of Christ to be brought to fullness in history. 'Grace supposes culture' means understanding that unity is 'multifaceted', a 'polyhedron' (*EG* 236) which assumes differences and separate components.

---

14 Cf. THOMAS AQUINAS, *Summa Theologiae* I, q.1, a.8.

This is valid both for the direction taken by inculturation (the different ways by which the peoples of the earth embody the faith within their cultures), and for how we understand the life of the people of God as such, how it develops in a particular place and time. Where the 'we' expresses a unity which maintains its diversity, as we have already said.

The visible and discriminating point for the unity of the People of God as such is, without any likelihood of ambiguity, its attitude to the poor, who are living indications of sacrifice and an appeal to quality of relationships. We are not speaking so much or only of 'helping the poor'. This would leave us at a necessary but insufficient point for recognising everyone to be citizens. We are talking about recognising that the poor evangelise us, that is, they show us by their lives, whether or not they are aware of it, the extent of our conformation to Christ. They need a gaze from us which recognises them (*EG* 48) and they offer a gaze which recognises us (*EG* 198).

If this relationship with the poor is a distinctive element of what it means to be the People of God, it is so because Christians are rooted in Christ, as also in the ancient and always relevant ways of believing throughout history: in their relationship with the Word of God, the sacraments, and especially the Eucharist, in shared prayer for one another, in the gestures of a daily faith which blesses and invokes.

There is a final necessary emphasis: to be a people requires a shared language which helps us be aware, helps us to share, makes our life recognisable and nurtures the new life which must result. Underlying this is the centrality of the *sensus fidei* and the *sensus fidelium*, the ability to recognise, listen to, decipher and diffuse the 'silent sound' of the believing life, the role this plays in Christian life and in building a sense of being a people.

This will be one of the places where the challenge of a new and more effective form of Church will come into play: we need everyone's subjectivity, theologians and common believers, magisterium and pastors, to find practices of expression of the sense of faith. For centuries we have gone down a one way path from a teaching Church to a learning one: this one-way approach is a mindset that needs to be surpassed. What is needed is to re-establish a virtuous circle of a mutual exchange of language.[15]

Perhaps this will be a place in which to begin to exercise the joyful labour of becoming a people

---

15 Cf. INTERNATIONAL THEOLOGICAL COMMISSION, *The 'sensus fidei' in the life of the Church* (13-07-2014).

through common responsibility, listening, word, humility and dignity, and in fraternal company with our pastors.

Andrew Downing, SJ

HISTORY AND THE OPEN HORIZON OF THE FUTURE

The election of Jorge Bergoglio to the papacy in 2013 brought with it a consciousness of history in the making. The first Pope in the history of the Church to be elected from the Americas, from the Southern Hemisphere and from the Society of Jesus vividly demonstrated the possibility of newness in an institution marked by ancient traditions and long memories. At the same time it brought to the See of Rome a pastor conscious of his task to speak to the Church and to the world in the current historical moment. That attention to the historical nature of Christian faith and life runs throughout the thought of Pope Francis and shapes the theology he presents in the growing body of his writings. It defines Christian faith as the lived encounter with the person of Jesus Christ. It sets the vocation of Christian life in context of collaboration with God's historical activity in the building of a more just world in the Kingdom of God. And it illumines the ground of Christian hope in the open horizon of the future to which the fulfilment of history is oriented. In each of these ways the Pope presents a theological understanding thoroughly informed by a consciousness of the importance of history for believing and living as a Christian in the world today.

From the writing of his first Encyclical, *Lumen Fidei*, Francis recognises how the Christian faith is bound to history and how that inherent connection relates to Christian hope. Itself something of an historical novelty, being promulgated by one Pope but drafted in some measure by his predecessor Benedict, the text sets out the basic structure of faith as an encounter with God, thus as a lived reality in the historical present, which is informed by past experience and oriented toward future fulfilment. As Francis acknowledges later in his second Encyclical *Evangelii Gaudium*: 'I never tire of repeating those words of Benedict XVI which take us to the very heart of the Gospel: "Being a Christian is not the result of an ethical choice or lofty idea, but the encounter with an event, a person, which gives life a new horizon and a decisive direction."'[1] It is a personal encounter with God in history that

---

[1] FRANCIS, Ap. Exhort. *Evangelii Gaudium*, 7; (24.11.2013); the quotation is taken from BENEDICT XVI, Encyc. *Deus Caritas Est* (25.12.2005), 1.

reveals God's love for us and for Creation, which in turn allows those who receive this gift of faith to see their lives in a new light and to imagine the possibility of a new history for themselves, as they live in response to that love. The model of this kind of faith is Abraham, who hears the word of God as a call to go forth from his home and to entrust his life to the promise made by God to receive a new home, in which the fullness of God's love may be known and lived. He bequeaths that faith to the people of Israel, a community always moving forward in faith toward its ultimate fulfilment by maintaining the memory of God's original promise to guide it along its way. Christian faith is formed in the same way, living as it does from the memory of the word spoken in Jesus Christ, whose Resurrection reveals the future promised made to all who believe. In this, 'we see how faith, as remembrance of the future, *memoria futuri*, is thus closely bound with hope,'[2] Francis writes, and it might added, we see the intrinsically historical nature of faith, as it reveals the full possibility of people's lives in the present by relating the present to God's action in the past and future.

The language of faith as a journey through history does not exhaust its description, however,

---

2 FRANCIS, Encyc., *Lumen Fidei*, (29-6-2013) 9.

and Francis, in the final chapter of *Lumen Fidei,* expands his discussion to speak of faith also as a truly collaborative project with God. Just as Israel's journey of faith did not continue forever in the desert but finally brought the people to the land promised by God so that they could build the holy city Jerusalem, so, too, may Christian faith be seen ' . . . also as a process of building, the preparing of a place in which human beings can dwell together with one another.'[3] Christianity is never lived alone but rather is always lived in a community, where the love God shares with us informs and animates the love shared between the members of that community. This love builds up the community of the Christian faithful, the Church, but as Francis insists, the community which Christians are called to help build today extends beyond the Church, too. The new society established in love, the New Jerusalem founded upon faith in the Resurrection, is a city that includes all people, involving social relations of every kind.[4] When people recognise the reality of God's love in the world and with that the true dignity of every

---

3   FRANCIS, Encyc., *Lumen Fidei*, (29-6-2013) 50.
4   'Faith does not merely grant interior firmness, a steadfast conviction on the part of the believer; it also sheds light on every human relationship because it is born of love and reflects God's own love. The God who is himself reliable gives us a city which is reliable.' FRANCIS *Lumen Fidei*, 50.

human person, they are able find the means to build on those foundations ever more just societies, where all may live in peace and security, according to laws and governance that serve the common good and what Francis describes in *Laudato Si'* as the 'authentic development'[5] of all their members. Then the social and political relations among people find their basis in true solidarity, allowing the possibility of forgiveness and reconciliation to emerge, and with those the growth of true unity beyond the mere absence of conflict. All of this requires time to come to fruition, indeed much time, and so with the use of the images of journeying and building to describe the Christian faith, Francis underscores its historical nature.

It is the second image of faith as the building of a new city, however, that allows Francis, in *Evangelii Gaudium,* to explore further the historical dimensions of the Christian faith in the present historical moment. The image of the city is particularly apt for this, since it at once expresses the long process of constructing human civilisation, begun literally with the construction of the first cities, as well as the situation of contemporary cultures, where so many dimensions of the existence of today's global community find their most acute expression.

---

5 FRANCIS, Encyc., *Laudato Si'*, 231.

In cities and in the urbanised cultures they nurture may be seen the great achievements of modern science and technology, on the one hand, along with the tragic consequences of those very achievements, on the other. The greatest possibilities for solidarity and common social action for human development exist beside the greatest disparities fostering political, social and economic marginalisation. To understand the significance of history in the present moment, then, one must understand the urban reality of so much of the world's population. From this context derive the myriad problems and challenges the world faces today 'amid the crisis of communal commitment,'[6] the nexus of political, economic, cultural and religious issues both the Christian community and societies at large must address, if the entire human family is to flourish. And here lies the great challenge, for the solutions to these problems do not lie solely in the Church but also in the midst of the complex reality of the city, i.e. the shared contemporary context of Christians and non-Christians, who are in different measures religious and secular, rich and poor, at the centre and at the periphery.[7] It is precisely there, Francis

---

6 FRANCIS, Apo. Exhort. *Evangelii Gaudium*, Chapter 2, title.

7 'It is curious that God's revelation tells us that the fullness of humanity and of history is realised in a city. We need to look

states, where, 'new cultures are constantly being born in these vast new expanses where Christians are no longer the customary interpreters or generators of meaning,'[8] that answers to the pressing questions of today are to be sought. Yet where the Gospel no longer forms - or never has formed - the basis of a particular culture, how are Christians to approach their newly configured task of discerning God's activity in such diverse circumstances and of evangelising their respective cultures?

Evangelii Gaudium discusses four 'principles' that emerge from the tensions present in contemporary society, which taken together present, if not a blue-print (Francis explicitly refuses this task![9]), at least a set of maxims to guide and encourage people today along the difficult way toward real unity. Each of the principles, derived from the Church's social teaching, might be seen in relation to an historically informed way of thinking, but key among the four is one the Pope first mentions in passing in *Lumen Fidei*: 'time is greater than

---

at our cities with a contemplative eye, a gaze of faith which sees God dwelling in their homes, in their streets and squares. God's presence accompanies the sincere efforts of individuals and groups to find encouragement and meaning in their lives.' FRANCIS *Evangelii Gaudium*, 71.

8   FRANCIS, Ap. Exhort. *Evangelii Gaudium*, 73.

9   FRANCIS, Ap. Exhort. *Evangelii Gaudium*, 51.

space.'[10] With this simple phrase Francis describes an underlying tension in historical existence: that which exists between life as one now experiences it and life as it could be lived, between the inescapable present moment and the as yet to be determined future. As he explains: 'broadly speaking, "time" has to do with fullness as an expression of the horizon which constantly opens before us, while each individual moment has to do with limitation as an expression of enclosure.'[11] The open horizon of the future becomes the reason for hope, for it lays before individuals the possibility that their lives - and their shared social life - can be different from the ones they have made for themselves, even as the difference between these two realities also reveals the distance yet to be travelled in order to attain that future. Thus Francis's remark is in one respect, at least, a counsel to take the long view of humanity's historical development and to exercise patience in the pursuit of that goal. Or considered from the other side of the tension, it advises against the all too typical emphasis in contemporary culture on 'space,' i.e. on '. . . madly attempting to keep

---

10   The four principles may be found in *Evangelii Gaudium*, 217-37. The reference to 'time is always much greater than space' may be also found in FRANCIS *Lumen Fidei*, 57.
11   FRANCIS, Ap. Exhort. *Evangelii Gaudium*, 222.

everything together in the present, trying to possess all the spaces of power and of self-assertion.'[12] The common human project of building a more just, secure home in the world, like the Christian project of collaborating with God's grace to build a new city, requires time and – more particularly – faith in the future fulfilment by others of efforts begun today.

That 'time is greater than space' is not simply an encouragement to persevere in the face of the slow course of progress, however. When seen in the light of the thought of Romano Guardini, a favourite author cited by Francis in every one of his encyclicals,[13] the principle becomes the basis both of a critique of the modern world as we know it and of the understanding of hope in the future of our world. 'Time' and 'space' figure significantly in the book *The End of the Modern World*,[14] in which Guardini offers a diagnosis of his contemporary context in terms of the waning of modernity and the emergence of a new culture with a quite different set of values and perspectives, for which Guardini seeks a name in his essay but what today would be called

---

12 FRANCIS, Ap. Exhort. *Evangelii Gaudium*, 223.
13 FRANCIS, Encyc. *Lumen Fidei*, 22; *Evangelii Gaudium*, 224; *Laudato Si'*, 105 (three references), 108 (two references), 203, 219.
14 R. GUARDINI, *Das Ende der Neuzeit* (Basel: Hess Verlag, 1950).

'post-modernity.' The modern age's fascination, even obsession, with 'space' for Guardini is a way of describing the technological reason that has come to characterise modernity. With modern science's discovery of a universe of infinite space, in which human beings inhabit but one tiny corner, comes the modern anxiety that humanity is no longer central to the universe and that its life has perhaps lost its essential value. To combat the growing suspicion of its own meaningless, modern culture employs its technological ingenuity to reshape the world around it, creating a space in which human beings can assert themselves and thereby impose meaning onto their own existence. Related to the modern desire to dominate space is a corollary sense of the modern age having lost its sense of 'time.' By this second term Guardini refers to how human cultures once possessed a richer historical perspective that allowed their members to see meaning and purpose in the course of their lives and in the life of the community. Christians were able to conceive of their lives as strands of the larger story of the Church and of humankind, making its journey through history from creation and redemption to final judgement. That knowledge bestowed on their lives an orientation within in a world also seen to possess meaning as the means for humanity's fulfilment. Modern day people in contrast know more and more facts about the world in which they live, but they no longer have the religious framework to give those facts meaning for their own existence or purpose. Without a sense of 'time,' neither humanity's origin nor its final end is made evident. As a result, the modern world, even with its many scientific and technological advances, has become fragile and threatened. Yet it is not without hope, for as Guardini remarks, 'contemporary man can bring himself to destruction . . . or he can fashion a new universal order, a space where he could fit himself and, conscious of human dignity, lay the roadway of the future.'[15]

To affirm that 'time is greater than space,' then, is far more than to simply accept the need for patience with the slow process of social or cultural development, or even to admit the importance of history as the place God encounters his people and thus where faith is lived out. Those elements are certainly true, and Francis speaks of them in his writings. But more profoundly, to grant priority to time over space is to engage in the kind of radical hope to which the Gospel calls, for it implies a turn to history and to dare to build there a new future,

---

15 R. GUARDINI, *The End of the Modern World* (London: Sheed & Ward, 1957), p. 114.

according to God's promise made in Christ. It is to reject the false promise of a future created by human technology and political ideologies, and instead to collaborate in God's plan revealed in the Resurrection to build a human community – a city – of reconciliation, solidarity and unity among all people. Today, that vocation resounds globally as a call to strive for the inclusion and development of the poor in the world community as well as to care for the planet, whose welfare is increasingly seen to be intimately bound to that of the human community living on it. Such is the clear message of *Laudato Si'*, but the same meaning and urgency run through all of Pope Francis's teachings, for they all share the vision of a world in which the destinies of all people are inextricably bound together – and bound to the destiny of Christ. Each of his encyclicals draws out different aspects of the same basic belief that the Christian faith finds in root in the historical encounter with God, its task in the historical situation of the present, and its hope in the as yet to be discovered future that God and his people will form together. In these ways Francis displays a style of theological reflection formed by an historical consciousness of the realities of the past and present, even as it remains open to the horizon of the future.

Nicolas Steeves SJ

'AN IMAGINATIVE POPE'S IMAGINATIVE THEOLOGY!'

It's clear as day that Pope Francis is a big fan of imagery. Try and count how many memorable metaphors his speeches employ. Think of the icons or statues of Our Lady he lovingly touches at the end of Mass. Consider how papal pictures and videos relay his iconic gestures and encounters. Critics, inevitably, will object and indict him for superficiality, media hype, and cult of personality... Nonetheless, all this imagery, in its diversity, proves highly successful with ordinary folks and the media. Just run a short, informal street poll about Pope Francis and people will give you a picture or metaphor of his which has inspired them.

How does this 'imaginative strategy' relate to theology? It is my opinion that *the imagination plays a fundamental role in theology*, and that *this statement fits Pope Francis' imaginative words and deeds like a glove*. To prove that point, let's describe briefly how he uses imagery, and then explain how these images are a true *locus theologicus*, i.e. the birthplace of real theological thought and practice. This 'imaginative theological colouring' of Pope Francis' magisterium will be shown to have some important sources and consequences.

Francis' extensive imagery: quick overview

It is not possible here to list each and every metaphor Jorge Bergoglio has used since becoming pope—a book would hardly suffice! Even a quick overview shows how extensively he uses imagery. Since March 2013, his daily *homilies at Casa Santa Marta* are his richest source of metaphors. To name just two that famously brought attention to his daily preaching: his rejection of a 'babysitter Church'[1] or a 'spray-on God'[2]. Another major source of memorable metaphors are his *interviews*. The main one Francis gave to Jesuit periodicals on August 19, 2013 is a cornucopia of similes that have become cornerstones of his pontificate: the 'Church as field hospital', or 'faith as a journey' instead of 'faith as a lab'[3].

---

1 FRANCIS, Morning Meditation in the Chapel of the *Domus Sanctae Marthae*, *The Church is not a Babysitter*, April 17, 2013.
2 FRANCIS, Morning Meditation in the Chapel of the *Domus Sanctae Marthae*, *The Divine is a person*, April 18, 2013.
3 FRANCIS, *Interview with Pope Francis* by FR ANTONIO SPADARO, August 19, 2013. Other metaphors in the same

'An imaginative Pope's imaginative theology!'

In our multimedia communications age, borne by wave after wave of one-liners, Francis' pithy analogies meet with great success and instant deployment. St. Peter's current successor clearly gets and *masters the codes of contemporary media communication* which rely fundamentally on images of all types, plastic and linguistic, real and virtual. Nothing is more 're-tweetable' than a well-honed metaphor, such as the one that pinned a 'pickled pepper face'[4] on surly Christians. Some Christians lament that the papal metaphors that get greatest social or mass media coverage are those that criticise or negatively typecast Catholics because they foster anticlericalism. It is definitely damaging (or at the very least reckless) to merely re-post the Holy Father's list of the Roman Curia's fifteen illnesses[5] while neglecting to subsequently republish the twelve virtues or cures[6] he offered in the following two years. Nonetheless, no one can deny how stimulating these papal metaphors should be for us Catholics, including those that are tougher

---

interview (such as "*machismo* in skirts" in the original Italian) were not re-used later on, perhaps for obvious reasons.

4 FRANCIS, Morning Meditation in the Chapel of the *Domus Sanctae Marthae*, *Melancholy is not Christian,* May 10, 2013.

5 FRANCIS, *Presentation of the Christmas Greetings to the Roman Curia*, December 22, 2014.

6 FRANCIS, *Presentation of the Christmas Greetings to the Roman Curia*, December 22, 2016.

and more challenging. We should, in fact, have as our first goal in life to heed Jesus' first public word, 'Repent!' (Mt 4:17). The Gospel's radical demands are a perfect fit for our ever-changing epoch: they rightly fuel Pope Francis's imagination so that it can craft striking words and deeds to meet today's overwhelming challenges[7].

Fundamentally, however, is this extensive imagery merely the fruit of crafty marketing tactics, or does it express any substantial theological depth? The Bible's exuberant imagery which comes to us in parables, metaphors, similes, narratives, poetry, visions, apocalypses, and more, strongly suggests the second answer. Theology and the imagination are deeply related to each other, for the sake of our salvation. Let us ground this thesis in Francis' writings[8].

---

7 This is the opinion, for instance, of the Rev. Julián Carrón, leader of the Catholic movement Communion and Liberation in the interview he gave J. Allen and I. San Martin on June 21, 2017 for the website *Crux*.

8 More could be said about how pictures or short videos of Pope Francis making significant gestures towards the poor and marginalized also lend theological credibility to the Petrine ministry, and to the Church, thanks to wide media broadcasting. It is a well-known fact that "a picture is worth a thousand words". This chapter, however, must limit its scope to the analysis of the current Bishop of Rome's written and oral speeches.

Images: a true *locus theologicus* for Pope Francis

A good starting point for our enquiry is the speech Francis gave to the community of '*La Civiltà Cattolica*' on February 9, 2017. Apart from its many metaphors, it offers a striking explanation of Francis' convictions about imagery. Take the last of the three thought-provoking words he gave the Jesuit review's writers: 'The third word [...] is IMAGINATION'[9]. Now, *Francis connects the imagination to discernment*—that practice so dear to Saint Ignatius Loyola's followers. Our imagination empowers us to 'penetrate ambiguity... just like the Lord Jesus when he took on our flesh.' The *Incarnation of the Word*: for Francis, this very dogma validates an imaginative moral and fundamental theology. Our imagination—the ability to receive and produce images—enables us to realise how much we follow Christ when we strive to reconcile opposites—God and man, time and eternity, principles and reality, and so on. This is the true ground for the *inseparable bond between the imagination and the Incarnation*[10].

---

9 FRANCIS, *Speech to the Community of "La Civiltà cattolica"*, February 9, 2017.
10 For in-depth reflection on this point, see N. STEEVES, *Grâce à l'imagination. Intégrer l'imagination en théologie fondamentale*, Paris 2016, especially in the conclusion.

This is why Francis 'like[s] poetry so much [... It] is full of metaphors. Understanding metaphors makes our thought nimble, insightful, flexible, and sharp. Imaginative people do not get stern or petty; they have a sense of humour and always enjoy the sweetness of mercy and inner freedom.'[11] Imaginative people can therefore follow Jesus, and with his grace, become for others an *alter Christus*, another Christ.

Herein lies the *raison d'être* of Pope Francis' magisterial endorsement of using imagery. When he suggests preaching imaginatively, *he is not endorsing cheap rhetorical tricks*[12]: 'An attractive image makes the message seem familiar, close to home, practical and related to everyday life. A successful image can make people savour the message, awaken a desire and move the will towards the Gospel.'[13] The purpose is to evangelise, to touch hearts so that people believe in Christ and thus act according to His Heart and Spirit. In fact, *an imaginative homily has a double impact, both cognitive and ethical.* The imagination

---

11 Francis, *Speech to the Community of "La Civiltà cattolica"*, February 9, 2017.
12 For more in-depth research on this point, see G. Piccolo – N. Steeves, *E io ti dico: immagina! L'arte difficile della predicazione*, Rome 2017, especially Chapters 2 and 5.
13 Francis, Apostolic Exhortation *Evangelii Gaudium*, November 24, 2013, 157.

allows Christians to enlarge their horizons, 'to imagine innovative spaces and possibilities for prayer and communion which are more attractive and meaningful[, especially] for city dwellers.'[14]

Francis, however, is no fool when it comes to possible misuses of the imagination, such as when 'we indulge in endless fantasies and we lose contact with the real lives and difficulties of our people.'[15] This Ignatian pope is well aware that the devil can fool us through the imagination's fantasising, or when it gets stuck in the rut of sterile, unrealistic brooding.

Despite all its possible shortcomings, however, the imagination is an indispensable means to lead the faithful to *true spiritual consolation*: 'In the homily, truth goes hand in hand with beauty and goodness. Far from dealing with abstract truths or cold syllogisms, it communicates the beauty of the images used by the Lord to encourage the practice of good. The memory of the faithful, like that of Mary, should overflow with the wondrous things done by God.'[16]

---

14 FRANCIS, Apostolic Exhortation *Evangelii Gaudium*, November 24, 2013, 73.
15 FRANCIS, Apostolic Exhortation *Evangelii Gaudium*, November 24, 2013, 96.
16 FRANCIS, Apostolic Exhortation *Evangelii Gaudium*, November 24, 2013, 142.

Beauty, goodness, and truth should chime in together to preach the 'Good News'[17] (Lk 4:18). Francis stressed this point in the 2017 Chrism Mass with the help of three 'icons' representing the 'joys of the Gospel': the 'stone water jars at the wedding feast of Cana', the 'jug [...] that the Samaritan woman carried on her head', and the 'fathomless vessel of the Lord's pierced Heart'. In his mind, the unimaginative preacher sadly misses a great chance to experience the joy of the Gospel and then share it with the faithful.

The backdrop to this theology of images and the imagination is both the Incarnation and another closely related mystery, the *creation of man*—the basis for a genuine *Trinitarian anthropology*: 'The very mystery of the Trinity reminds us that we have been created in the image of that divine communion, and so we cannot achieve fulfilment or salvation

---

17 FRANCIS, *Homily for the Chrism Mass, April 13, 2017*. By a beautiful stroke of luck, the Preface to the same Mass reads: "For Christ [...] with a brother's kindness also chooses men to become sharers in his sacred ministry through the laying on of hands. [...] As they give up their life for you and for the salvation of their brothers and sisters they strive to be conformed to the image of Christ himself". If all men and women are created in the image and likeness of God, priests have the additional task of conforming themselves to the image of Christ. Such imaginative theological musings have clearly been feeding Pope Francis' priestly and episcopal ministry all along and made him imaginative, too.

purely by our own efforts.'[18] The claim that we are created in God's image and likeness (Gen 1:26) is thus yet another source for the pope's theology of imagination.[19]

It follows that, if we are created in this image and likeness, our imagination must mirror that of God. Divine *Revelation* must touch our imagination to revitalise it and to bring it back to reality. All too often, alas, it strays towards fantasyland or quits that 'serious game' which God entrusted to it—reconciling opposites. Only God's creative Revelation can make the human imagination 'keep it real'. Accordingly, the *faith* this imaginative Revelation elicits in us must also become creative in exercising *charity* concretely, against the eschatological horizon of *hope*, by peacefully, joyfully professing the truth. Divine Revelation and faith, it should be noted, always move across *human cultures in their variety*. These three elements—Revelation, faith, and culture—form the basis of a *genuine fundamental theology of the imagination*. Pope Francis yearns for this 'third word[,] IMAGINATION' to turn our

---

[18] Francis, Apostolic Exhortation *Evangelii Gaudium*, November 24, 2013, 178.
[19] For more in-depth research on this point, see M. Tenace, *Dire l'uomo. Dall'immagine alla somiglianza, la salvezza come divinizzazione*, Rome 2015, especially Chapters 1 and 3.

Christian lives towards the joyous proclamation of the Gospel.

Obviously, his imaginative fundamental theology draws water from several sources. Let us now explore them before sketching out some last touches on the consequences of an imaginative theology.

Sources and consequences of Francis' imaginative theology

Clearly, a first source of Francis' imaginative fundamental theology is the creative German-Italian theologian R. Guardini. The young Fr Bergoglio started doctoral research work on him before being sent back to Argentina on another mission. Guardini's *The Spirit of the Liturgy* and *Sacred Signs* offer many a beautiful page describing how liturgical gestures, objects, and symbols not only elicit faith in those who partake in the celebrations, but also efficiently rescue modern man from the twin pits of rationalism and sentimentalism[20].

Another clear source of Pope Francis' imaginative theology is the *Bible*, which overflows with all kinds of imagery. Bergoglio, as a Jesuit,

---

20   See R. Guardini, *The Spirit of the Liturgy*, New York 1935; *Sacred Signs*, St. Louis 1956.

'An imaginative Pope's imaginative theology!'

also enhances the impact of Biblical imagery through the prayer methods St. Ignatius Loyola offers in the *Spiritual Exercises*. By meditating and contemplating Gospel scenes, and especially by 'applying the senses'[21], Ignatius helps us harness our imagination so that it leads us to God. Ignatius' use of the imagination is not geared towards escaping reality. Quite the opposite, actually. The *Spiritual Exercises* use the imagination to penetrate reality so as to discern God's concrete will and to decide to endorse it and make it happen here and now. How much Pope Francis uses highly imaginative Ignatian discernment methods shines through in *the ways how he decides and acts*, whether by prayer and personal decision on the basis of inner conviction, or by a more rational decision after thinking things out on his own or consulting others[22]. If you use an imaginative theology, you can actually learn from others, too, according to how they receive your imagery and react to it.

A consequence of the theological role Francis grants to imagery and the imagination is his welcoming appreciation of a certain *plurality in the hermeneutics of Revelation*, as long as it is respectfully consistent. A merely conceptual theology, by

---

21 See IGNATIUS LOYOLA, *Spiritual Exercises*, [121]-[126].
22 See IGNATIUS LOYOLA, *Spiritual Exercises*, [175]-[189].

contrast, does not allow for diversified hermeneutics. Obviously, his way of proceeding may upset those endowed with a more notional or systematic mindset. But Jesus of Nazareth almost always spoke in parables or metaphors, as did the prophets of old or St. Paul. The Church's Magisterium also proceeds likewise. For instance, the Second Vatican Council's Constitution *Lumen Gentium* speaks of the Church using ten different metaphors[23] because *such a great mystery cannot be caged in tightly sealed conceptual systems*.

On a final note, let us add that no imaginative theology holds without constantly *discerning* whether new interpretations of the divine Revelation respect both the Gospel and reality. Such a theology must also *steer clear of hardening or fossilising metaphors*. If pastors, theologians, and the faithful wish to honour Pope Francis' way of carrying out theology (regarding both content and method), they must always let *their own imagination be moved and be made fruitful by divine grace in the cultures where they seek to live out the Gospel*. Doing likewise would indeed be an instance of true 'creative fidelity'![24]

---

23 See *Catechism of the Catholic Church*, 753-757.
24 For more in-depth research on this point, see G. MARCEL,"La fidélité créatrice" in *Revue internationale de philosophie*, 2/5, 1939-1948, pp. 90-115.

Gerard Whelan SJ

POPE FRANCIS' THEOLOGICAL METHOD

In a short book, *Pope Francis' Revolution of Tenderness and Love*,[1] Cardinal Walter Kasper notes that Pope Francis is not a trained, professional academic, whereas his two predecessors were (Pope John Paul II had been a philosophy professor, Pope Benedict XVI a theology professor). He suggests that there is no particular reason why popes should be academic professionals, but adds that when they are not, there emerges a particular role for those who are: they need to interpret the significance of the teaching of such a pope to the academy. In this light, he identifies the goal of his book: 'to approach the Francis phenomenon theologically and to illuminate somewhat the theological background and the theological substance of his pontificate.' He expresses his conviction that 'new perspectives are emerging' in the pontificate of Francis and sets out

---

[1] W. Kasper, *Pope Francis' Revolution of Tenderness and Love* (Mahwah, New Jersey, USA: 2015).

to demonstrate this. For example, he explains that there exists a key difference between Pope Francis and his predecessor Pope Benedict; however he adds: 'it does not concern theological truth. Rather it concerns *theological method and its concomitant emphases*.'[2]

In what follows, I suggest that Pope Francis' method of doing theology has three major characteristics: it is rooted in a notion of discernment drawn from the *Spiritual Exercises* of St. Ignatius; it adopts the inductive style of the 'See-Judge-Act' method; and it employs a preferential option for the poor. I then identify three consequences of the Pope employing this method: criticism of abstract ideologies, the appeal to a process of dialogue, and the opposition it has provoked in certain quarters.

Discernment

Early in his pontificate, Pope Francis gave an interview to a Jesuit journal where he makes it clear that the notion of discernment, as understood in the *Spiritual Exercises* of St. Ignatius, is central to his approach to life.[3] To fully understand the meaning

---

2 IBID. 7, 12.
3 When Pope Francis is asked, 'What element of Ignatian spirituality helps you live your ministry?' He answers, 'discernment,' and adds: 'Discernment is one of the things

of the term discernment in Ignatian spirituality, one needs to have undergone the experience of the *Spiritual Exercises*, which are normally offered in the form of a thirty-day silent retreat under the guidance of a director whom you meet every day. In fact, the booklet known as *The Spiritual Exercises* of St. Ignatius is a manual to guide the director in his or her guidance of a retreatant. Briefly put, discernment of spirits helps individuals differentiate between interior states of consolation and desolation and to become confident that decisions made in times of consolation are likely to be consistent with the will of God. The *Spiritual Exercises* helps to school individuals in practising this method of self-awareness in a way that is intense, subtle, and which can form the habit of a lifetime. This leads individuals to take a process-oriented approach to life, something Ignatius describes as being 'contemplatives in action.'

Those familiar with an Ignatian notion of discernment recognise how deeply the interview Pope Francis gave in November 2013 reveals him to be a contemplative in action. He describes how

---

that worked inside St Ignatius. For him it is an instrument of struggle in order to know the Lord and follow him more closely.' A. SPADARO, Pope Francis, interview, August 2013, 'Who is Jorge Bergoglio?' http://americamagazine.org/pope-interview.

'the wisdom of discernment redeems the necessary ambiguity of life,' and adds that it is a humbling experience and helps one adopt means for decision-making that 'do not always coincide with what looks great and strong.' With remarkable honesty he speaks about mistakes he made in his life. He notes that he was required to carry responsibility in Jesuit governance when he was too young to do so. He describes how he behaved in 'an authoritarian and quick manner' that led him to have serious problems. Having learnt his lesson, he speaks of how he learnt to become more consultative and adds that, now, 'I am wary of the first decision, that is the first thing that comes into my mind when I make a decision. This is usually the wrong thing.'[4]

Pope Francis also explains how Ignatian spirituality expands naturally to a philosophy of knowing that, in turn, influences one's approach to a world of pastoral concerns. When offering advice to his fellow Jesuits, he states: 'The Jesuit must be a person whose thought is incomplete, in the sense of open-ended thinking.' He adds: 'Discernment is always done in the presence of the Lord, looking at the signs, listening to the things that happen, the feeling of the people, especially the poor.' Reference

---

4   A. Spadaro, Interview, 3

to issues such as the signs of the times and the importance of listening carefully to the poor, brings him beyond questions that appertain strictly to Ignatian discernment and on to broader questions of pastoral-decision making.

Inductive method

Jorge Bergoglio was ordained priest in 1968, and so was pursuing theology studies during the years of Vatican II.[5] He learnt the significance of the call by Pope John XIII, in the opening speech of the Council, for the event to be 'pastoral' and not primarily doctrinal. His teachers explained that such a pastoral attitude implied adopting an inductive approach to theology, one that contrasted with the primarily deductive approach of the Neo-Scholastic theology that had predominated in the Church before this time. They explained that this move toward the inductive method had its origins in a practice of pastoral decision-making pioneered by Fr Joseph Cardjin in the early-twentieth-century Belgium. Cardjin had spoken of a method of 'See, Judge, Act.' Over time, this method had come to

---

5 Biographical comments on Jorge Bergoglio made in this work are based on A. IVEREIGH: *The Great Reformer: Francis and the Making of a Radical Pope* (London, Allen & Unwin: 2014).

be recognised as having a relevance for how the whole of theology might be done. In 1961, it had received explicit support from Pope John XXIII in his encyclical, *Mater et Magister*.[6]

Bergoglio learnt that key examples of an inductive method at work in the Council were found in two of its four major documents, or constitutions. In the first, the Dogmatic Constitution on the Church, *Lumen Gentium*, where the Church is described as the People of God. By use of this image, the Church is understood as an actor in history, a fellow-traveller with the rest of the human race. The second document was the Pastoral Constitution, *Gaudium et Spes*. Here the use of the method of 'See-Judge-Act' is most evident. The document begins with a study of the World context in which the Church is called to minister; from there it moves to a reflection on the way that the Gospel answers the deepest yearnings of modern men and women; in conclusion, it explores ways in which the Church should engage with issues such as: family life; of social justice; and peaceful international relations.

---

6   Joseph Cardijn founded the movement 'Young Christian Workers' in Belgium in the early twentieth century (see, *Joseph Cardijn, Challenge To Action,* Edited by Eugene Langdale [Chicago IL: Fides Publishers, 1955]). Pope John XXIII expresses approval of this pastoral method in *Mater et Magister* (15 May 1961, paragraph 236).

In the early years of his priesthood, Bergoglio witnessed the emergence of a distinctively Argentine theology, which focused on how to apply Vatican II to the particular circumstances of that country. Beginning with the inductive moment, 'See,' this theology noted that particular characteristics of their country included poverty, inequality of wealth, political oppression, and a rich popular culture including particular forms of religious expression. Moving to the stage, 'Judge,' it drew on on the theme of the Church as People of God to describe the poor masses of Argentina as representing an example of this notion. Moving to the stage, 'Act,' it made various pastoral proposals for how the Church could both support the religious culture of the poor and help direct it to have an end that included social transformation in Argentina. This school of theology became known as the *teología del pueblo* and was recognised as a form of liberation theology that was different from those emerging in other countries of Latin America, in that it made less use of Marxist analysis.

As a Jesuit Novice Master, Provincial Superior, and Rector of a college of philosophy and theology, Bergoglio had opportunities to reflect about the links between Ignatian spirituality and the *teología* *del pueblo.*⁷ He began to articulate his vision in the form of four pastoral principles, principles which he retained when he was appointed Archbishop of Buenos Aires and which he reiterates as Pope, for example in his Apostolic Exhortation, *Evangelii Gaudium*.⁸

The first principle is that 'time is greater than space.' Here he stresses the importance of patience in trying to address the 'processes of people-building.' The second principle, is 'unity prevails over conflict.' Here he addresses the reality that in any community conflict will arise. He suggests that 'conflict cannot be ignored or concealed,' but adds that neither should we become so obsessed with conflict as to become 'prisoners to it.' He suggests that the appropriate stance is to try to 'face conflict head on, to resolve it and to make it a link in the chain of a new process.' A third principle is 'realities are more important than ideas.' Here he criticises tendencies to abstract and universalising thinking

---

7   An important explanation of the intellectual roots of Pope Francis is offered by his former philosopher lecturer, Juan Carlos Scannone, in 'Papa Francesco e La Teologia del Popolo' (*La Civiltà Cattolica*, 3930, 15 Marzo 2014, Anno 165, 571-590). This section I also rely on unpublished talks and round-table discussions from a conference run jointly by *La Civiltà Cattolica* and the Pontifical Gregorian University, March 27-28, 2014, 'Le radici di Papa Francesco. Un anno di Pontificato,' in which Scannone took part.

8   FRANCIS, *Evangelii Gaudium*, 224-234.

suggesting: 'ideas – conceptual elaborations – are at the service of communication, understanding, and praxis.' A fourth principle is 'the whole is greater than the parts.' Here he suggests 'an innate tension also exists between globalisation and localisation.' He proposes that we both pay attention to the global 'so as to avoid narrowness and banality' and to the local 'which keeps our feet on the ground.'

A preferential option for the poor

Pope Francis never tires of stating that a discerning, open-minded, approach to pastoral decision-making must always attend to the concerns of the poor. In *Evangelii Gaudium*, he states:

> This is why I want a Church which is poor and for the poor. They have much to teach us. Not only do they share in the *sensus fidei*, but in their difficulties they know the suffering Christ. We need to let ourselves be evangelised by them. . . . We are called to find Christ in them, to lend our voice to their causes, but also to be their friends, to listen to them, to speak for them and to embrace the mysterious wisdom which God wishes to share with us through them.[9]

---

9 FRANCIS, *Evangelii Gaudium*, 198: http://w2.vatican.va/content/francesco/en/apost_exhortations/documents/papa-francesco_esortazione-ap_20131124_evangelii-gaudium.html

In this quotation a number of characteristics are to be noted. Pope Francis is moving beyond a call to express solidarity with the poor by being present to them and offering help. He is affirming the importance of letting their concerns dominate the way that theologians conduct their craft. On this issue, Pope Francis takes care to distinguish his position from a Marxist one. This is part of the reason why he expresses his conviction that the poor possess a 'mysterious wisdom.'

A characteristic of a more Marxist approach to liberation theology was to suggest that the poor did not know how to think for themselves and that their culture was merely the 'false consciousness of the ruling class.' Consequently, such thinkers spoke of the need for theologians, and other elite figures, to help direct the energies of the poor toward a revolutionary praxis as called for by a Marxist theory of history.[10] Bergoglio opposes such thinking emphatically. He acknowledges that theologians must give voice to the concerns of the

---

10   SCANNONE in, 'Papa Francesco e La Teologia del Popolo,' points to the following liberation theologian as propounding what is essentially a Marxist-Leninist approach to liberation and as offering direct criticism of the new Argentine *teología del pueblo*: J.L. SEGUNDO *The Liberation of Theology* (English translation of original publication of 1974, New York, Orbis Press, 1976), 'Theology and Popular Religion,' 196-200.

poor in a form that is more sophisticated what they can articulate. However, he suggests that it is fundamentally disrespectful of the poor to impose abstract solutions on them that derive from Marxist theory. He states:

> The poor person, when loved, 'is esteemed as of great value', and this is what makes the authentic option for the poor differ from any other ideology, from any attempt to exploit the poor for one's own personal or political interest. Only on the basis of this real and sincere closeness can we properly accompany the poor on their path of liberation.[11]

When Bergoglio was appointed as Archbishop of Buenos Aries, he found himself thrown onto a situation where he was obliged to comment on national affairs. Here he witnessed the sometimes corrupt practices of certain politicians, and did not hesitate to denounce them. Also, he witnessed a collapse of the Argentine economy, in 2002. He believed this to have been caused, not primarily by corruption in local politics, but by the loyal application of principles of neo-liberal economics which the international community had obliged the Argentine government to follow. This led him

---

11 FRANCIS, *Evangelii Gaudium*, 199.

to denounce such economic theories as another example of abstract thinking, disconnected from context, that results in oppressing the poor.

As Pope, Francis has made a major contribution to Catholic social teaching by extending it to the question of the environment. Furthermore, a characteristic of *Laudato Si'* that many commentators find striking is the manner in which it employs a preferential option for the poor to reflect upon the ecological issue. Here we note that the title for the letter is taken from a hymn of praise of St. Francis of Assisi that praises God through God's creation. Now the Pope, who takes his name from this saint, suggests that it is St. Francis of Assisi who: 'shows us just how inseparable the bond is between concern for nature, justice for the poor, commitment to society, and interior peace.' In introducing the encyclical, he adds:

> I will point to the intimate relationship between the poor and the fragility of the planet, the conviction that everything in the world is connected, the critique of new paradigms and forms of power derived from technology, the call to seek other ways of understanding the economy and progress.[12]

---

12   FRANCIS, *Laudato Si'*, 16.

Consequences of using this method

I would now like to point to three consequences of Pope Francis' use of the theological method I have been outlining.

The first consequence is that Bergoglio is strongly opposed to anything he considers to be an abstract and ideological way of thinking. He considers this to be a mistaken way of guiding personal and social activity, one that causes further harm to the poor. Throughout his life, the Pontiff has been able to identify three ways in which this abstract thinking has been expressed: a certain approach to theology typical of the preconciliar mentality and Neo-Scholastic theology; Marxism; and some forms of neo-liberal economy.

The second consequence of the Pope's method is the constant appeal he makes to processes of dialogue, often described as a call to the "culture of encounter". This approach is needed both when speaking of certain issues *ad intra* to the Church and when making reference to statements *ad extra*, such as the Church's mission in the world. On the *ad intra* question of Church governance, Pope Francis draws on the notion of collegiality that is expressed in

Lumen Gentium.[13] One of the first steps he took after his election was to appoint a group of eight cardinal advisers who would help him reflect on all aspects of his ministry. In *Evangelii Gaudium* he offers intense criticism of clericalism and over-centralisation in Church governance, and raises the question of a change in Canon law to give more power to episcopal conferences of bishops. His Apostolic Exhortation *Amoris Laetitia*, on family life, is also the product of a new and collegial approach. This was evident with regard to the Synods of bishops that led up to this apostolic exhortation. This included sending out questionnaires to all the dioceses of the world before synods; the calling of two synods rather than one; and the procedure within the synods of holding small-group discussions (rather than basing Synods on a series of long lectures by a small number of high Churchmen).

Amoris Laetitia is not only the result of a collegial approach. Its content testifies to the presence of a principle regarding dialogue. Many Catholics are only able to give imperfect witness to the Church's teaching on sexuality and marriage. Therefore, the Pope suggests that pastors enter into dialogue with Catholic couples so that gradually

---

13   Cf. VATICAN COUNCIL II, Dogmatic Constitution on the Church, *Lumen Gentium*, (21-11-1964), 22.

they can live out the Christian message more fully. In suggesting this pastoral practice he appeals to the principle of gradualism in theology, a principle that highlights the importance of small steps.

When Pope Francis addresses *ad extra* questions, one recognises that he does not pretend to be able to propose detailed solutions to world problems; rather, he proposes processes of inclusive dialogue that can help to produce such solutions. The main conclusion of *Laudato Si'* is a call for five processes of dialogue: within the international community; at the level of national and local politics; for 'transparency in decision-making'; between economics and politics; and between religions and science.[14]

A third consequence in the use of this method is that it provokes opposition in certain quarters. He has experienced opposition from various groups during his lifetime. In general, this opposition has really come from people belonging to the ideologies he has criticised. When he was a young Jesuit, this opposition was strongly influenced by Marxist thinking As Archbishop, he was hindered especially by people who belonged to the neo-liberal current. And now, as Pope, it seems the obstruction comes especially from people in the higher echelons of Church.

---

14   FRANCIS, *Laudato Si'*, Chapter 5.

How do we explain this opposition, fed within Church walls? It must be acknowledged that the method of this Pope differs from that of his two predecessors. The pastoral and theological approach of both Pope Saint John Paul II and Pope Benedict XVI was more deductive than inductive.[15] Combined, these Popes were in office for thirty-five years, so it is not surprising that a significant change in policy would come as a surprise to many. But surprise is one thing, opposition another. The latter has arisen precisely against Pope Francis' approach. The opposition, instead of preferring dialogue, is constantly on the lookout for clear and abstract statements on so many questions of a moral nature.

One might speculate that there is a certain irony to be witnessed regarding those who make public criticisms of the Pope's policies. Might they not be recognised as those whom the Pope judges to be affected by "spiritual worldliness"? The Pope's reflections on this are strong and sharp,[16] but I believe that more urgent issues are emerging.

---

15 Cf. W. KASPER, *Pope Francis' Revolution of Tenderness and Love*, 11. See also, M. FAGGIOLI, *Pope Francis, Tradition in Transition* (Mahwah, NJ: Paulist Press, 2013).

16 In *Evangelii Gaudium* the Pope speaks of a 'spiritual worldliness.' He suggests that this worldliness, 'hides behind the appearance of piety and even love for the Church.' He adds

Conclusion: called to change horizons

As already stated in the introduction, Cardinal Kasper asserts that with Pope Francis, 'new things are emerging' and essentially this concerns theological method. This is why theologians have the task of explaining these new things to an academic audience. I believe I can I can offer some suggestions. Bernard Lonergan's reflection in *Method in Theology* (1972) can clarify some aspects of Pope Francis' teaching.[17]

According to Lonergan, the challenge in modern theology consists of transforming "a classic mentality into historical consciousness." This means, first of all, a transformation of the horizon of theologians from "a theoretically differentiated consciousness" to an "inwardly differentiated consciousness." In Lonergan's opinion, the real novelty of the Second Vatican Council consisted of this transformation that began to present itself in a more substantial way. He maintained that this change, even though it had begun, was not yet complete and this is even the case in a document like *Gaudium et Spes*, where another historical consciousness predominated. Therefore, it would be

---

that this can express itself in 'an ostentatious preoccupation for the liturgy, for doctrine and for the Church's prestige. FRANCIS, *Evangelii Gaudium*, 93, 95.

17 Cf. B.F.J. LONERGAN,

important to continue in the footsteps of *Gaudium et Spes* to tackle future pastoral challenges. According to me, Pope Francis' inductive and existentialist method is what Lonergan would have hoped for. Everything that Lonergan says regarding method in theology explains very well the direction that Pope Francis has sought to impress on his reflection.[18]

Also, in my view, using a Lonergan type perspective allows us to understand the resistance that the figure of Pope Francis given rise to in certain quarters. He is asking for a transformation of horizons: from a more risky abstract classicist and guaranteed view, marked by historical consciousness. In this latter, it is possible to identify the tensions that arise when, for example, we want to be faithful to a religious tradition, or want to listen to the signs of the times, or when we reflect on how we should develop the tradition and how certain pastoral practices should change. People of good will, too, could note the threat of a similar change of horizon. During the Second Vatican Council, one *peritus*, in perfect harmony with Lonergan's analysis of the Council, explicitly backed his position. John Courtney Murray played an important role in the

---

18 Cf. G. WHELAN, "Theological Method in *Evangelii Gaudium*. A Dialogue with Bernard Lonergan and Robert Doran", *Gregorianum 96/1 (2015) 51-57*.

drafting of the "Declaration on Religious Freedom, *Dignitatis Humanae*". At a certain point he wrote an article to defend the draft document circulating among the Council Fathers. He spoke about a "first view" that hindered religious freedom and a "second view" that favoured it. He had realised that the debate between these two positions was rigid and sought to explain it, employing Lonergan's categories:

"This abortive dialogue seems to indicate where the real issue lies. The First and Second View do not confront each other as affirmation confronts negation. Their differences are at a deeper level indeed, at a level so deep that it would be difficult to go deeper. They represent *the contemporary clash between classicism and historical consciousness*."[19]

It is possible to identify a strict parallelism between those who oppose Pope Francis and the tensions that Courtney Murray had noted during the Second Vatican Council. I truly believe that Pope Francis' theological method represents the transformation of a paradigmatic way of conceiving the Pontiff's teaching and is in profound continuity with the Second Vatican Council. It is all disturbing.

---

19 J.C. MURRAY, *The Problem of Religious Freedom*, Woodstock Papers 1965, 7. The italics have been added, quoted by G. WHELAN, "John Courtney Murray and 'The Contemporary Clash between Classicism and Historical Counsciousness'", *Gregorianum* 97/3 (2016) 486.

What the Pope teaches is branded as "new things" because this is the first Pontiff to have such a marked historical consciousness. His desire is to be faithful to the spirit of the Council and to point out the way for the future.

James Corkery, SJ

FRANCIS, HEIR AND INNOVATOR: AN ARGENTINIAN POPE AND JESUIT IN THE POST-CONCILIAR TRADITION

Introduction

Popes can be written about in different ways. One of these is to take a 'great men' approach, which views the history of the papacy in terms of remarkable personalities who have put their own particular stamp on the Church and the world. There is enough about Pope Francis that is distinctive to warrant such an approach in his case. He is from Argentina, the first pope from the continent of Latin America. He is a Jesuit, the first also. He follows in the tradition of his post-conciliar predecessors, John Paul II and Benedict XVI, yet he diverges from them also, particularly in how he speaks and acts. Francis is the first fully post-conciliar pope; he did not attend Vatican II and he studied theology after it had finished (1967-1970). Also he is not, like Benedict

XVI and John Paul II, a diocesan priest, but rather a member of a religious order, the first since Gregory XVI, a Camaldolese monk, who became pope in 1831. Francis's immediate predecessors were academics, one a professor of philosophy, the other of theology, but he spent most of his life as a pastor, in important leadership roles. First he was provincial of the Jesuits in Argentina, subsequently auxiliary bishop, then archbishop, and finally, universal pastor, Bishop of Rome. Taking a 'great men' approach to his papacy could draw on several of these distinctive aspects of Francis's life in order to highlight what makes him different; but it would miss aspects that result from his standing in a line of popes at a particular time in history. No pope appears entirely 'out of the blue;' his historical situation shapes his papacy, just as his papacy shapes his historical situation; he inherits, he innovates.[1] Thus the focus in this chapter will be on Francis both as *heir* – receiver of a tradition – and as *innovator* – a person who responds creatively to that which he has received.

---

[1] Cf. J. CORKERY - T. WORCESTER, eds, *The Papacy Since 1500: From Italian Prince to Universal Pastor* (UK and New York: Cambridge University Press, 2010), the Conclusion especially (pp. 243-251).

Francis in the tradition of the post-conciliar popes

There have been, since the time of the Second Vatican Council, four popes prior to the present one: Paul VI (1963-1978); John Paul I (August 26, 1978 – September 28, 1978); John Paul II (1978-2005) and Benedict XVI (2005-2013). Francis bears the stamp of each of them. Paul VI's apostolic exhortation, *Evangelii Nuntiandi* (*EN*), published while he was provincial of the Jesuits in Argentina and when liberation theology was growing rapidly in prominence in Latin America, influenced him. *EN*'s treatment of human and social 'liberation' as integral to evangelisation, but as only part of the fullness of salvation in Jesus Christ that the Church's faith proclaims,[2] was significant for the theological approach that he took in the 1970s when some Jesuits of the Argentine Province's Centre for Social Research and Action (CIAS) were espousing a line that was close to the theology of liberation. Furthermore, *EN*'s influence is evident in Francis's own exhortation on evangelisation some forty years later; he refers to his predecessor some dozen times. In his second apostolic exhortation, *Amoris Laetitia* (*AL*), Francis again stands in the tradition of Paul VI

---

2 See PAUL VI, *Evangelii Nuntiandi,* nos 29-38 especially. The text is available at www.vatican.va (last accessed on July 8, 2017).

when he highlights, drawing on the *Relatio Synodi* of 2014, how in his Encyclical, *Humanae Vitae* (*HV*), Paul VI 'brought out the intrinsic bond between conjugal love and the generation of life' (*AL* 68). There is repeated allusion to *HV* in *AL*.

Paul VI was a pope *of* and *after* the Council. Of the three popes who followed him before the election of Francis in 2013, the first, John Paul I, reigned for just thirty-three days. He once referred to God as 'mother', and this is perhaps echoed in Pope Francis who, in writing about 'tenderness' in relation to God's mercy, points to a rich Hebrew vocabulary that is maternal in character as lying at the root of what tenderness means.[3] In the case of John Paul II, however, there are unmistakable echoes of his magisterium in the writings of Francis. This is not only the case in *Evangelii Gaudium* (*EG*), a text speckled with references to a very wide range of John Paul II's teachings, but John Paul II is also prominent in Francis's apostolic exhortation, *AL*, where his catecheses on sexuality and his 1981 apostolic exhortation on the role of the Christian Family in

---

3   On his use of 'mother', see JOHN PAUL I, *Angelus*, September 10, 1978 (last accessed at www.vatican.va on Wednesday July 5, 2017). See also: POPE FRANCIS, *General Audience* on "The Mercy of God," January 13, 2016 (last accessed at www.vatican.va on July 11, 2017); and see Francis's bull, *Misericordiae Vultus* (11 April 2015), no. 6.

the Modern World, *Familiaris Consortio* (*FC*), are repeatedly in evidence, even if Pope Francis's method in *AL*, with its strong emphasis on discernment and accompaniment, is markedly different from that of Pope John Paul II in *FC*. The connection between these two popes lies not only in continuities in their teaching, however; it is personal also. It was John Paul II who appointed Jorge Bergoglio an auxiliary bishop in 1992, coadjutor archbishop in 1997 (and Archbishop of Buenos Aires a year later). In 2001 he made him a cardinal.

Francis's immediate predecessor, Benedict XVI, has been praised and quoted by him repeatedly since the beginning of his papacy in 2013.[4] In *EG*, the first major document to come exclusively from Francis, he refers to Benedict's now famous words in *Deus Caritas Est* (*DCE*) about an encounter with Jesus Christ standing at the very centre of Christian faith; and Francis adds: 'I never tire of repeating these words of Benedict XVI which take us to the very heart of the Gospel' (*EG* 7). Benedict is also prominent in several other places in *EG*,

---

4 See *Address of His Holiness Pope Francis on the Occasion of the Inauguration of the Bust in Honour of Pope Benedict XVI* (hereafter *Inauguration*) given at the Plenary Session of the Pontifical Academy of Sciences on Monday 27 October 2014 (last accessed at www.vatican.va on 5 July, 2017). See also, for example, EG, 7 and AL, 70, 147, 157, 164, 186.

with Francis continuing to draw especially on his first encyclical, *DCE*, and also on his third, which deals with integral human development in charity and truth, *Caritas in Veritate* (*CV*). Francis, in his remarks about 'human ecology' in *Laudato Sì* (*LS*), builds on what Benedict said (at the *Bundestag* in 2011, and elsewhere). He allies himself also with Benedict's view that belief in creation and accepting evolution are not contradictory.[5] Several other examples can be found in the writings of Francis that reveal him to be an heir to the tradition of Benedict. However, as with his inheriting from John Paul II, there are many differences between Francis and Benedict also, particularly in method, language and style – above all in ecclesiological matters. This will become clear as we turn now to examine Pope Francis under the aspect of innovator.

Francis the innovator – what exactly is he doing?

Following thirty five years of the combined papacies of John Paul II and Benedict XVI, the latter

---

5 On 'human ecology,' see D. HOWARD SJ, "*Laudato sì*: a Seismic Event in Dialogue between the Catholic Church and Ecology," in: *Thinking Faith: The Online Journal of the Jesuits in Britain* (www.thinkingfaith.org, last accessed on July 11, 2017), p. 1. On "creation/evolution," see *Inauguration*.

having begun with the remark that he had no wish to issue many new documents of his own but only to ensure the assimilation of those of his predecessor,[6] an innovator has become the Bishop of Rome. In what do his innovations consist? I will attempt to identify and present a few: first, a shift in ecclesiology; second, a retrieval of neglected perspectives – that of the poor and that of the Church in dialogue once again with the world; third a re-balancing of the Second Vatican Council's two Constitutions on the Church, *Lumen Gentium* and *Gaudium et Spes*; fourth, operating under the influence of his Jesuit background – in how he governs and in recalling 'a faith that does justice;' fifth, doing theology in a new key.

An ecclesiological shift

With Pope Francis, an ecclesiological shift is occurring. It is his view of the Church that makes him different and – people are right – this does not involve a change in doctrine, but a change in language, style and emphasis, a change that brings with it a new image of the Church itself. 'The image of the Church I like is that of the holy, faithful people

---

[6] See D. GIBSON, *The Rule of Benedict: Pope Benedict XVI and his Battle with the Modern World* (San Francisco: HarperSanFrancisco, 2006), p. 248.

of God,' he said, in an interview with the editor of *La Civiltà Cattolica* less than half a year into his papacy.[7] 'The Church is the totality of God's people.' It is this people 'on the journey through history, with joys and sorrows' (Interview). Here Pope Francis is sketching a picture of the Church, even when attempting to say what it is. He offers an image rather than a definition – not even a definition using the concept of 'communio,' so often on the lips of his predecessor, not only while he was pope but also while he was Prefect of the Congregation for the Doctrine of the Faith.

It is not that Francis rejects the concept of 'communio,' but precisely because it is a concept he sidesteps in favour of a more concrete focus. His image of the Church as a 'field hospital,' treating the injured, binding up wounds, showing endless mercy and compassion, is a vivid one that has stayed in people's minds. He prefers to say what the Church does rather than what it is. The first chapter of *EG*, entitled 'The Church's Missionary Transformation,' speaks also of what the Church does. It 'goes forth.' As a community of missionary disciples, the Church goes out. 'I dream of a missionary option,'

---

[7] Interview with Pope Francis by A. Spadaro, available under heading "Discorsi" at www.vatican.va in Italian from *L'Osservatore Romano*, 21 September 2013, and also in English translation (hereafter "Interview").

Francis writes, 'a missionary impulse capable of transforming everything, so that the Church's customs, ways of doing things, times and schedules, language and structures can be suitably channelled for the evangelisation of today's world rather than for her self-preservation' (*EG* 27). This means change, conversion, a reality that begins with each person – 'the first reform must be the attitude,' he says, unfolding his field hospital image. And each person is involved, the pope too, for the papacy must also be converted and renewed (*EG* 32). In all this, there is a shift of focus from how the Church is to be understood (theology) to how it must act (pastoral engagement).

Retrieving neglected perspectives

Pope Francis is engaging in theology here, looking at the Church's faith in a new way, based on a conscious closeness to the perspective of the poor and on a retrieval of neglected elements from the Second Vatican Council such as synodality, dialogue with the world, and collegiality with his fellow bishops. He consults the faithful broadly, as in the preparatory work carried out for the Synods on the family and the eventual publication of *AL*. He seeks to dialogue with the whole world about the future of the planet: 'In this Encyclical, I would like to enter into dialogue with all people about our common home' (*LS* 3). Further on, he says: 'We need a conversation that includes everyone' (*LS* 14). He sees *LS* as a call to conversion to everyone, inside and outside the Church. He has retrieved the forgotten point in *Gaudium et Spes* 44 about how the Church learns from the world as well as the world from the Church; the *ecclesia discens* is once again in the picture. Finally, Francis involves his fellow bishops more in his governance of the Church and in his teaching, as his appointment of a group of diverse cardinals from around the world to assist him indicates and as his frequent citing of bishops' conferences' documents from every continent also demonstrates. There is innovation here, fresh acting. The Italian theologian, Severino Dianich, sees in Francis's way of acting a change in style, a change in the forms and methods of the magisterium.[8] Francis is teaching, not by changing doctrine, but by exploring, presenting and applying it in a new way, seeking above all to make it helpful and life-giving in pastoral situations. The Church should act as a loving parent – father, mother (*EG* 46-49, *AL* 308) – and good parents do not drive children away.

---

8 Cf. S. DIANICH, *Magistero in Movimento: il caso papa Francesco* (EDB, 2016).

Re-balancing the two Constitutions on the Church

It was said above that Pope Francis's theological and magisterial approach involved the retrieval of certain elements that became obscured with the passage of time, including recent time, such as aspects of *Gaudium et Spes*. From the Extraordinary Synod of Bishops called by Pope John Paul II in 1985 to mark the 20th anniversary of the Council, and for the twenty remaining years of his papacy, followed by the almost eight-year papacy of Benedict XVI, the central ecclesiological concept in papal and magisterial teaching on the Church has been that of 'communio.' And the viewpoint that the Council's teaching on the Church is best summed up in the notion of 'communio' led to a focus, in reflection on the ecclesiology of the Council, almost entirely on its Dogmatic Constitution on the Church, *Lumen Gentium*, as if there were not also another one, the Pastoral Constitution, *Gaudium et Spes*, the main concern of which was the Church's relationship with the world, which is very much the focus of Francis, who sees the Church above all as missionary. An ecclesiology centred on the notion of *communio* did not need to turn aside from *Gaudium et Spes*, of course, but this in fact is what happened. And

Francis is redressing this balance. Therefore, while not ignoring *Lumen Gentium* in his ecclesiology by any means, he is clearly more oriented to *Gaudium et Spes*. During Benedict's papacy he directed much of his attention to the Church *ad intra*, but Francis's focus is on the Church *ad extra*. Benedict did not use images for the Church that were drawn from outside of its traditions but Francis speaks of the Church as a 'field hospital,' as a *Church going forth*, as a 'missionary disciple' (*EG* 40) and he is impatient with a Church that thinks or talks too much about itself (what he calls a 'self-referential' Church). So, although both popes draw freely on the ecclesiology of Vatican Council II, they draw on it differently, and it is interesting that Francis, just ten years younger than Benedict and a product in every way of the post-conciliar Church, marks something of a new generation in popes: at once traditional and new; at once heir and innovator! Some of this newness may come from the fact that he is a Jesuit also.

Influenced by his Jesuit background

In being a Jesuit, Francis also represents a way of proceeding different from that of his papal predecessors. For example, he uses some Jesuit practices in governing the Church, like having a close circle of cardinal-advisors from far-flung places – these are like the consultors of a Provincial – and not from within the Roman curial structure. This represents a certain decentralisation, as does Francis's choice of cardinals, in a different way. He quite frequently chooses them not from the world's centres of power: Baltimore (the primatial see in the U.S.), Philadelphia, and other expected cities, but rather from countries like Bangladesh, Laos and Capo Verde. And he chooses many who have a proven track-record in serving the poor. The poor stand very visibly at the centre of his ministry, both in many of the places he chooses to visit (Lampedusa, to take his very first example) and in how they are prioritised wherever he visits (example, Washington). He rejects symbols of wealth and power, preferring a small car to a large one, choosing to live in St. Martha's rather than in the Apostolic Palace (although he claims this is because he needs community). He has improved the conditions for the homeless in Rome, above all near the Vatican. Francis may not be a 'liberation theologian,' but he is a theologian of the liberation of the poor, the sick and the marginalised. He lives with the words of his friend, the Brazilian, Cardinal Hummes, ringing in his ears since he was elected: 'Don't forget the poor.' The fact that he has not, means also that, as Pope, he has been innovative –and faithful also to the option for a faith that does justice that was embraced by the Society of Jesus in its 32nd General Congregation in 1975, which Father Bergoglio attended.

Theology in a new key

Pope Francis is different from his immediate predecessor in the manner in which he avails of and engages in theology also. Pope Benedict XVI crafted his texts with academic exactness and careful attention to detail. Francis, less academically exigent, it is true, says that our thought must always remain somewhat unfinished, always be open to completion, and that a closed system that leaves no room for creativity is a travesty of what good theology is. His encyclicals and apostolic exhortations exhibit this. Their language is not conceptual and he speaks often in categories that are personal and relational (*AL*, LS) and engaging, inspiring (*EG*). His is the language of a pastor who has been where people have been, has asked them what they think, and has listened to their answers. He prefers a fresh, concrete, realistic and image-rich language that is based on his actual pastoral experience and on his closeness to priests rather than a language that only educated people can understand.

Francis underscores and draws on popular piety (*EG* 122-126). He sees it as a *locus* for theological discernment. Discernment tries to take everything into account. As a procedure, an art, it requires a gathering of information about, and a thinking and praying on, concrete realities. It asks for reflection, in the light of God's word, on actual situations that present themselves. It seeks to discover what God's will is, not in the abstract, but in the particular circumstances in which decisions must be taken. Thus it does not admit of a 'one size fits all' approach to moral and social teaching. However, this makes many people nervous; they are more at home, for example, with John Paul II's clarity in *FC* 84 than with Francis's journey of discernment in *AL*, chapter 8 (in relation to discerning the possibility of giving communion to some divorced and remarried persons). Both approaches to moral decision-making have their supports in Christian and Catholic tradition, but it would be flying in the face of the facts to say that Pope Francis does not prefer one over the other. He does. And this makes, has made, and will continue to make 'waves' in his innovative, yet faithful, papacy.

www.ingramcontent.com/pod-product-compliance
Lightning Source LLC
Chambersburg PA
CBHW072044290426
44110CB00014B/1568